Trail and
Mountain Running

Trail and Mountain Running

Sarah Rowell and Wendy Dodds

THE CROWOOD PRESS

First published in 2013 by
The Crowood Press Ltd
Ramsbury, Marlborough
Wiltshire SN8 2HR

www.crowood.com

British Library Cataloguing-in-Publication Data
A catalogue record for this book is available from the British Library.

ISBN 978 1 84797 455 6

Acknowledgments
The authors would like to thank the following for giving their time and expertise to help shape the contents of the book:

Bob Smith, Mark Townsend, Barbara Lonsdale and Hilary Bloor for their insightful and challenging questions and suggestions throughout; Dr Steve Ingham for advice on the training sections; Ian Holmes, Jez Bragg and Jonathan Wyatt for sharing their training ideas and plans; Ali Rose and the staff at the Coach House Physiotherapy Clinic for their assistance and expertise with the exercises included in the book (and for helping keep Sarah Rowell running); those who have let us use their photos, in particular Triss Kenny, Dave Woodhead, Andy Holden, Ian Charters (www.justusuk.com) and Dan Vernon; your work really brings our words to life.

We would also like to thank all those other friends who have given us advice and shared many days on the hills over the years, and who have provided us with the inspiration for this book; and, last but not least, our long-suffering partners Andy and Ralph for their help, support and patience.

Picture on page 2 courtesy Berghaus.

Typeset by Phoenix Typesetting, Auldgirth, Dumfriesshire

Printed and bound in India by Replika Press Pvt Ltd

CONTENTS

ABOUT THE AUTHORS

Sarah Rowell

Sarah started running during the early 1980s marathon boom, winning gold at the World Student Games in 1983 (where Wendy was one of the medical staff), representing Great Britain in the 1984 Olympic marathon and setting her personal best of 2.28.06 when finishing second in the 1985 London marathon.

Injury issues meant that her focus switched to off-road surfaces. In 1986 she won the Seven Sisters marathon outright, becoming the first woman to achieve such a feat. In 1992 she finished second in the World Mountain Running Championships, and in 1996 and 1997 she won the British and English fell-running championships. More recently she has focused on longer events and running for pleasure.

In normal life Sarah works as an advisor within high-performance sport and is the team leader for UK Athletics mountain running. She also advises a number of athletes, from recreational to international.

Wendy Dodds

Wendy diversified from being a junior international swimmer and an orienteer as a student, taking up mountain running in 1972 when she did her first Mountain Marathon. Over the years she has run regularly over the fells with numerous age-group English and British championship wins, though favouring long races. She won her age group category in the first five years of the Runfurther Trail race series and in 2006 was third FV50 in the UTMB.

In parallel with her running she has been a Sports Physician for over thirty years working with many sports, being a Team GB doctor at four Olympic Games and a volunteer doctor at London 2012. In retirement she has been able to be a full-time athlete(!), allowing her to reproduce times from twenty years ago when training was limited by professional commitments.

Sarah and Wendy first teamed up in 1991 to break the women's record at the Haworth Hobble, previously held by two Olympic marathon runners (Angie Payne and Veronique Marot), with their time still being very respectable twenty years later. More recently they have formed a consistently successful Mountain Marathon partnership.

FOREWORD

My introduction to off-road running – or more specifically, fell running – came when I stood in a muddy field in Yorkshire one wet evening many years ago watching 100 or so runners revelling in the panting, sweating, rough 'n' tumble joys of testing themselves to their limits whilst getting soaked, battered and cacked-up… and still managing to smile and laugh at the finish.

Since then I've been so obsessively steeped in this huge world of trail and mountain running – a memory bank full of fells, mountains, forests and fields – that I've practically forgotten how it felt to start; to leave the pavement behind and discover all those paths, trails and open moorlands. Which of course is where a book like this would have come in handy.

Within a few months of publishing a book about wild (off-road in all its variations) running, the most common enquiry I had from road runners were variations on the theme of 'Where do you start?' We're so used to the city centre marathon as a symbol of modern running that we sometimes can't

see the woods for the trees, don't understand where to look, what to wear, how to train and prepare … in short, we need some friendly advice from someone who's spent the better part of a lifetime learning the dos, don'ts, how-tos and how-not-tos of the sport.

In this there can't be many better, more reassuring voices at your side than Sarah and Wendy, two women whose knowledge of fell and mountain races has been gathered over the years by running, racing and training over every corner of this windswept or sun-beaten, craggy or grassy, storm-soaked or bracken-dry country of ours.

On the assumption you don't live next door to Sarah and Wendy, do yourself a favour and get yourself a copy of this book. Use it as a guide to discovering – safely – a new and exciting world full of possibilities. Then go and have fun!

Boff Whalley
Author of Run Wild

INTRODUCTION

Who is Trail and Mountain Running for?

Running, it could be argued, is the most natural form of exercise. For all its simplicity, there are many books, magazines and websites giving advice on how to run faster, train better, avoid injuries and how to maximally support a running habit. Why then another book, especially one focused on trail and mountain running, which are often described as pure and that you 'just do'? If it is that simple, why devote a whole book to them? This is a good question and for some runners a book such as this is not needed, as they already have the confidence, experience and skills to run on trails and mountains happily, safely and successfully. Those runners are, however, in the minority. There are many more who want to progress with their running, whether it is racing for the first time; venturing from roads on to trails and mountain paths; moving from running 10km to longer distances and even ultras; or wanting to feel confident about being able to run safely in more isolated environments. It could also be that they are simply open to finding out more, in order to improve their performance.

It is for these runners that this book has been written, in which we share the knowledge and insights we have gained through a combined seventy years' (plus) worth of experiences, running and coaching; and over which professional careers are layered, ensuring that the practical advice provided on the following pages is grounded in current medical and scientific best practice.

The Enjoyment of Running

For both of us, running has been interwoven into our lives. It has and continues, on a near daily basis, to provide us with the enjoyment to be gained from putting one foot in front of the other, with a feeling of body and mind in harmony. On a good day, you have one of those runs where all seems effortless and you seem to float along at speed. It provides an environment where your brain seems to function optimally, your mind coming alive, buzzing and on fire, generating ideas, solving problems and composing the most eloquent of text. Conversely, there are the days when your run perhaps is a bit of a plod, feeling more of a struggle, but one after which you still feel better on your return home, maybe cheered by the sight of deer or other local wildlife. Yes, there are the times when injuries or poor form mean you question the physical and emotional time and effort invested, but, if you are training smartly, these occasions are far outweighed by the good times.

Running, and in particular racing, has also provided both of us with much pride and satisfaction as goals set out at the beginning of the year are focused on, trained for and achieved. Not always: for both of us there have been targets that have 'got away' and have had to be added to the 'reflect, learn and do differently next time' box. While the

The enjoyment of running off the beaten track. ANDY HOLDEN

former aspects (goals accomplished, titles, positions or times achieved and races won) are the ones most of us strive for, it is the latter from which we often learn more.

Running and racing are much more than focused competition and aiming to win – after all, it is only a very few in each race who get called up on to the podium. This does not stop the fun of having goals and a focus for running, whether it is beating the person who always beats you, finishing in the top half of the field, being faster than the last time or a totally non-race related target – running further, somewhere new, staying fit and healthy with age. This book is a running-focused and carefully planned dissemination of our experience and knowledge, designed to help you increase your enjoyment of running off the beaten track, whatever your goals.

Trail and Mountain Running

What do we mean by trail and mountain running? It is a pretty broad description. What types of surfaces, events and distances does it cover? And, perhaps just as importantly, what, in the context of this book, does it not cover? Historically, long-distance running, and certainly racing, mainly took place on roads and paved surfaces. There have always been some exceptions to this, such as the Orion 15, which was first held in 1954, but until relatively recently, British distance running races were predominantly on hard surfaces. Fell running (often called hill running in Scotland) is the exception to this, with races, which date back to 1870s, being held over quite extreme terrain. Likewise, in Continental Europe and America there is a long history of mountain (Europe) and trail (USA) races being held.

Pendle: a traditional fell race. ANDY HOLDEN

More recent times have seen a surge of interest in running and racing on non-paved surfaces, both in the UK and abroad. Increased road traffic, increased costs, more restrictive policing requirements, better maps, wanting a different challenge, enjoying a more pleasant environment: these are just some of the reasons linked to this shift.

Trail and Mountain Running provides advice relevant to trail, mountain and fell races. While it is possible to roughly differentiate between the three types of race, in practice it is not so simple as many races do not neatly fit into one box or the other. As this book is all about running off-road, an activity which in itself is more unstructured compared with the rigid demands of the road, so much the better. For the purposes, therefore, only of helping readers apply the information and concepts in this book to their own training and racing, the following definitions will be used:

A fell race is over rough off-path ground, does not normally have a marked or set route (allowing for route choice), visits one or more hill summits or checkpoints, requires runners to be self-sufficient, and meets the race categorization criteria of the Fell Runners Association, kit often having to be carried.

A trail race is mainly on trails/paths/tracks, the route may or may not be marked but does not normally allow route choice, there are usually aid stations at checkpoints, may or may not be hilly, kit may or may not be required to be carried.

A mountain race is on well-marked single tracks or wider trails/four-wheel-drive tracks; if in Europe is often uphill only or has more uphill than down, has a considerable amount of ascent, has aid stations if a longer race, has a marked route with no route choice.

All three types of event include races lasting anything from ten minutes to over five hours.

As can be seen, the potential for overlap between the types of event is considerable. For example, a 10km trail race might be accurate in distance, well marked, have a fast, flat surface and great for decent times (that is, more akin to a road race); on the other hand, it may be on rough ground, approximately measured, on a muddy, twisty and hilly course (verging on being a fell race).

There are other forms of running taking place off-road: in particular, pure cross-country and orienteering events. Trail and mountain running often require similar skills and expertise to these, but neither cross-country, orienteering nor other challenge or multi-skill events such as adventure racing will be covered by this book.

Grossglockner mountain race, Austria. TRISS KENNY

How the Book is Structured

Trail and Mountain Running is not designed as a complete guide to running and training as there are already plenty of books that do that well. We make the assumption that readers have some knowledge of training and already do some running; our book is not designed for those who want to start running. Rather, its focus is on those runners who want to progress, whether that be running and racing off-road for the first time, getting faster or better at trail or mountain running, tackling a new, longer distance or challenge, or just running safely in a harsher environment.

The book is divided into three parts. The first, Training Fundamentals, contains five chapters, which will provide you with all you need to know to be able to run and train for trail and mountain running, covering how to:

- Plan an appropriate training programme.
- Optimize your training programme for off-road running.
- Supplement your running training to maximize performance and minimize injury risk.
- Be able to enjoy and be safe in non-urban environments.
- Look after your body most effectively; ensure you have appropriate shoes and kit for the conditions.

The second part, Racing, is about competing and covers the key areas runners need to be aware of if they want to race successfully on trails and mountains. There are three chapters in this section, covering in order:

- *Pre-race preparation* – including kit, tapering and mental preparation.
- *Racing* – including what to carry, race tactics, fuelling and pacing.

- *Post-race* – including refuelling, warming down and recovery techniques.

The final part is Optimizing Performance. If the first part covers the foundations of successful running on trails and mountains, then this final part is about making sure that all options are covered to maximize perform-ance for the specific event or environment you want to run in. The three chapters here cover:

- How to make use of cross-training methods whether you are injured or not.
- The final I per cent – the little things to think about when all else has been covered.
- How to race well all season.

As noted previously, there are myriad different types of mountain, trail and fell running races and events, which means different training and preparation require-ments are needed for each. Throughout the book, especially in the Taking your Training Off-Road chapter and the Racing section, four stereotypical races will be used as examples:

1. *A 45min fell race* – a classic British fell race, going to the top of a hill and back down where there is off-path running; the race route is unmarked; runners can choose their own route.
2. *A 70- to 90min mountain race* – a typical European-style race, with lots of uphill running; on decent trails and paths; the race route is marked.
3. *A 3- to 4hr trail race* – on a mixture of undulating trails, grasslands, paths, bits of roads, the race checkpoints must be visited, allowing some route choice but it may be a marked or flagged route, some support en route provided.

The leaders in the 2012 Great Trail Race. DAN VERNON/NOVA INTERNATIONAL

4. *A 10hr-plus ultra race* – on a mix of undu-lating trails/grasslands, paths, roads, the race route must be followed but it is not marked, some support en route provided at the checkpoints.

Using these four races as examples will allow us to show how training and race preparation should best be altered depending on the length and nature of the event you are preparing for.

There are few pages at the end of the book in which you can jot down key points, notes and other things of use to you.

PART I

TRAINING FUNDAMENTALS

The first of three sections, Training Fundamentals gives you all the knowledge you need to run off-road in terms of training programmes, looking after your body, kit and equipment and staying safe in the environment

ANDY HOLDEN

CHAPTER I

UNDERSTANDING TRAINING

Putting together a training programme for running (or any sport) is potentially very simple – you just get out and run. While this may work for some, it is, to use a cooking analogy, a bit like throwing a set of ingredients together to make a cake with no considera-tion as to the ingredients, the quantities, in what order, how to mix, how long to cook for, at what temperature and how long to cool before eating – if you are lucky it may work out really well, but there is a significant risk of ending up with a sticky mess.

To maximize improvement, there are various things that need to be taken into consideration. Staying roughly with the cake-baking analogy: just as there are thousands of different (sometimes subtly, sometimes signif-icantly different) recipes for cakes, all of which result in a tasty outcome, so there is a similar range of training programmes. Training is not an exact science, with only one right way; rather, it is a case of blending the key parts together in a way that suits the individual runner and their aims – the key is making sure that all the critical variables are in sync.

The variables are as follows:

- The race or target: what is the event being trained for and what is the result wanted?
- The basic training principles: what we know about how the body responds to training.
- The individual runner: their physiology, anatomy and psychology will all influence what the best training programme is.

- The different types of training.
- The runner's current lifestyle.
- The chronological and training age of the runner.

Influencing how these come together is the specific training philosophy adopted. All these variables must be carefully blended in the right way at the right time to create the overall successful training programme or recipe. As with a cake, get any part of the process wrong and the outcome will not be the best.

As an example, it is not uncommon to see running Internet forums hosting whole pages of debate about how long or how fast long runs should be – here the only correct answer is, 'it depends'. The question is like asking how many bananas need to go into a banana cake and should they be mashed or sliced: impos-sible to answer without the context of the overall recipe (or training plan).

On the one hand, designing a training programme can appear to be quite complex and hence it appears easier for many just to follow a ready-made recipe. On the other hand , if you have a basic understanding of the key principles and the way various ingredients work in different circumstances, then you have the tools either to tailor existing training programmes (like those in this book) to fit your personal circumstances, or to make your own programme from scratch. Both of these latter approaches will result in a personalized fit-for-purpose training programme, one that you will enjoy more and find easier to follow and should bring about a better end performance.

Before considering the practical nuts and bolts of training programmes for our four featured events, first we need to have a quick reminder of the basic principles of training. This is followed by a look at why we train. What are the main training principles that help us go faster and the types of training that will be most effective? Once we have all these, we are in a position to marry all the pieces together to produce effective training programmes. These programmes are covered in Chapter 2, where there is a section simply called 'Ideas to Try' with some recommendations for training sessions we have used successfully.

Principles of Training

Individuality Everyone is different: everyone starts with a different genetic make-up, has a different lifestyle, a different ability to adapt and respond to training; training programmes must therefore be tailored to best suit individual runners.

Specificity What you train is what you improve: that is to say, the adaptations our bodies make to training are highly specific to the load placed on them (this is not to denigrate cross-training, which is covered in Chapter 10).

Overload To improve something you have to progressively provide a greater stress than the body is used to. Once the body becomes used to a specific load, training needs to be changed to provide a greater stress or overload in order to continue to improve.

Off-road runners come in all shapes and sizes. DAVE WOODHEAD

> **Reversibility** Use it or lose it, all training adaptations are reversible, and while it is not true that if you do not run for a week you lose half your fitness, if you stop any form of training for any length of time your training gains will reverse.
>
> **Hard/Easy** Whether via days, weeks or larger training cycles, optimal training gains are made by mixing hard training with rest/recovery phases. There is much truth in the concept that it is during the easy/recovery training phases that the fitness adaptations from the hard training are gained.

Why Train?

Some runners train simply because they enjoy the experience of running, the satisfaction of the post-run physical ache and tiredness, or the emotional runner's high. Most, however, also train to get better or, once you reach a certain age, to slow down the natural decline in performance that comes with age.

How does training help make us go faster? What are the key adaptations that training aims to bring about to ensure that this occurs? If we know what we are aiming to positively change in terms of physiological function or anatomical structure, and we know what types of training best bring about this change, then we have a logical reasoning on which to design a training programme.

Physiological training adaptations can be broadly categorized into three interrelated areas:

- Optimizing energy and power production.
- Running economy.
- Running effectiveness.

In addition, there is mental strength: the ability to focus on the task in hand, to struggle through the bad bits and to refocus when things go wrong. This whole area will be looked at in more detail in Chapter 11.

Energy Systems

Much of what is written about training programmes focuses on increasing the delivery of usable energy to the working muscles; in other words, developing the cardiovascular system. This is as critical to trail, mountain, and fell running as to other forms of endurance activity.

Your body's potential energy comes mainly from three sources: fat, carbohydrate and ATP. Fat and carbohydrate are stored in the body as triglyceride and glycogen respectively and in longer events can be obtained from food or drink consumed. ATP, or adenosine triphosphate, is the carrier of energy that the body uses to release energy to the working muscle. Put another way, all energy from food is trapped by ATP before it is released when required. During exercise your body's metabolic processes drive the resynthesis of ATP to continue to release energy. The body can also use protein as a source of energy; however, this only really occurs when the body is depleted in carbohydrate.

In simple terms, the body has four different options available to it to turn potential energy into usable energy and then generate power and movement. Of these options, three are most important in the context of this book.

The ATP-PCr System Used to support very quick, maximal bouts of movement lasting up to around 6–10 seconds, this system is independent of oxygen and occurs via the breakdown of molecules of stored ATP and PCr (phosphocreatine), allowing the muscle to generate force quickly. For endurance runners, this energy source will only really come into play in the final sprint for the finish line and is the least important for trail, mountain and fell runners.

The Glycolytic or Anaerobic System This resynthesizes ATP independently of oxygen (hence the term anaerobic, or 'without oxygen') and because it does not use oxygen, it can generate energy quickly as the body breaks down stored glycogen to re-synthesize ATP. One of the by-products of this system is lactic acid, which can accumulate if the intensity is too high for too long and it is associated with excessive metabolic muscle fatigue.

The generation of lactic acid is not in itself a bad thing; rather, it is a natural part of how the body generates useable energy. In normal circumstances (namely, when there is enough oxygen around), there is a shuttle system in action, whereby lactic acid is created by the working muscles and then shuttled to either adjacent muscle fibres or to the liver to be reconverted back into a useable energy source. As the body works harder (that is, you run faster), the level of circulating lactic acid rises (because it is being generated at a faster rate than can be shuttled away and reconverted) until a point at which accumulation of metabolic by-products, in particular hydrogen ions, interferes with muscle contraction – or the feedback to the brain from a burning sensation in the muscles convinces you to ease up.

A person's lactate threshold (lactate turn-point or anaerobic threshold are other terms commonly used) is the point (or speed) beyond which an increase in exercise intensity results in a rise in the circulating level of lactate and acidity, that if allowed to increase excessively leads to eventual fatigue.

Training for the glycolytic system focuses on positively influencing two things: first, increasing the body's ability to tolerate a higher level of circulating lactate before inhibition occurs and, second, increasing the ability to generate and recycle lactate so that for any given speed the circulating lactate level is lower.

The Oxidative Glycolytic and Oxidative Lipolytic Systems Many texts consider the oxidative systems as one system; however, when considering the range of endurance events and the different training effects, that there are two different sources of energy involved, merits thinking about them separately. Put simply, both oxidative systems require oxygen to resynthesize ATP and enable movement. The oxidative glycolytic system releases the body's more limited stores of energy in glycogen (stored carbohydrate) or circulating glucose for ATP and can do this quite effectively in terms of the amount of ATP generated per unit of oxygen used. The oxidative (lipolytic) system, on the other hand, generates ATP from the breakdown of lipids or fat. While your potential 'fat' energy pot is much greater, the energy released is more expensive per unit of oxygen than that for carbohydrate/glycogen (and hence tends to mean slower movement).

In reality, the body uses both these systems concurrently. The harder it is working (or faster it is moving), the greater the amount of energy coming from glycogen compared to lipid. However, the pot of available glycogen is limited and when this runs low, energy production and hence speed reduces as the body becomes much more reliant on breaking down fats to release energy to resynthesize the required ATP. (The most obvious effect of this is 'hitting the wall' when running a marathon.)

For endurance runners, training these systems is focused on increasing the capacity of the body to convert the fuel stores to energy (that is, to achieve a higher conversion rate), as well as increasing the body's ability to use fats as an energy source. Typically, faster marathon and ultra runners use a higher percentage of fat compared to carbohydrate to generate energy for a given speed. This in turn prolongs the length of time they can maintain their speed before glycogen stores run out.

Table 1: Summary of Energy Systems

Name	Energy Generation	Lasts for	Events when used
The ATP-PCr system	Stored ATP and PCr	6–10sec	Sprints
The glycolytic or anaerobic system	Generates ATP from stored glycogen without using oxygen.	Up to 30min	Main energy source for 45min fell race. Important energy source for a 90min mountain race.
The oxidative glycolytic system	Generates ATP from stored carbohydrate (glycogen) using oxygen.	90–120min	Main energy source for a 90min mountain race. Key energy source for 3hr trail race.
The oxidative lipolytic system	Generates ATP from stored fat using oxygen.	Longer than 90min	Important energy source for a 3hr trail race. Main energy source for 10hr ultra race.

Running Economy

While the ability of the cardiovascular system to deliver usable energy to the muscles and of the muscles subsequently to contract is important, their relative importance in the overall scheme of running faster in endurance events is a moot point. It is well established that if you were to measure the effectiveness of the cardiovascular system using a measure known as the maximal oxygen uptake (the maximum amount of oxygen the body can take in via the lungs, transport via the heart and cardiovascular system and uptake at the muscle – often considered the best overall measure of cardiovascular fitness), in all the runners in a particular endurance race there will be a strong correlation between the faster the runner and the higher the maximal oxygen uptake. However, if you were to take the top 10 per cent of the race field or all the finalists in an Olympic Games 10,000m race, then the relationship between maximal oxygen update and performance becomes much more tenuous.

Why? Because movement efficiency or running economy is just as important, if not more so, in influencing the performance outcome. If maximal oxygen uptake is the maximum amount of oxygen that the body can transport to the working muscles, then running economy is a measure of the amount of oxygen required to run at any given speed; that is, the higher the running economy, the higher the speed you can run while using the same amount of oxygen, as opposed to the absolute highest speed. Typically (but not always), the best endurance athletes – certainly those running distances of 10km and over – are also the most economical, but not necessarily those with the highest maximal oxygen uptake.

The great thing for runners is that running economy has a strong positive association with training in that by practising running the body becomes more economical at running. Indeed, most runners probably have just as great a potential to improve their running economy as they do their pure cardiovascular fitness.

Running Effectiveness

What do we mean by this? What exactly is running effectiveness? If optimizing energy and power production is about ensuring that there is maximum energy available (think of the engine and fuel delivery system in a car), then running effectiveness refers to the ability of the lower limbs (in the case of running) to use this available energy as efficiently as possible. For runners, this in particular relates to the optimal functioning of the key pivots at the foot/ankle joint and the pelvis.

Running effectiveness is critical for all runners, but even more so for trail, mountain and fell running ones where the ability to maintain speed over rough and uneven ground, ideally without an increase in effort, can make the difference between a good and a great performance. We can probably all think of great road runners who, once running off-road and on anything other than smooth trails, suddenly start to struggle and their previous smooth stride becomes one of apparent uncoordinated stuttering. Looking a little deeper, running effectiveness has three main components:

Local Muscle Strength and Fatigability Muscles are made up of numerous muscle fibres. Muscle movement occurs via the coupling and uncoupling of small cross bridges (think little hooks) between the fibres. Fatigue within the coupling process, particularly in ultra events, will mean that even in the presence of enough useable energy the muscle contraction (the end result of all the individual fibres moving across each other) will not be as strong or as fast.

Local Elasticity and Contractibility Muscles are attached to bone via tendons, which operate a little like mechanical springs, absorbing force as well as storing and transferring elastic energy as you land and take off when running. Ligaments provide stability to joints and are of a similar composition to tendons. All three – muscles, tendons and ligaments – with age and use, are susceptible to declining elasticity or contractibility (think

of an old frayed elastic band). Just as an old rusty spring is a bit tight and does not spring back so well, in the same way the bounce and spring afforded by older well-used soft tissues decline. When this happens, it not only adversely affects running economy, but also the force and shock impact on the rest of the body is potentially increased.

Neuromuscular Efficiency and Optimal Firing Movement is generated by messages (or impulses) sent from the brain via nerves to the muscles, each nerve connecting with a number of muscle fibres. Optimal movement happens when all of the required muscle fibres contract in sync, time and force wise. This is something that specific running drills (covered in Chapter 3), if done correctly, can help improve. Post-injury, it is often the case that this recruitment is out of sync, but here again the use of functionally based drills will help correct matters.

Interlinking of the Physiological Adaptations

In reality, all three areas above are integrated: improve your cardiovascular fitness and it will positively impact on your lactate threshold, and this in turn will boost your running economy. Lose the elasticity and responsiveness in the lower-limb ligaments and musclo-tendinous units and your running economy will decrease irrespective of your cardiovascular fitness or the muscles' local ability to recycle and shuttle lactic acid.

Consider a real-life example (always also remembering people respond differently to the same training stimulus). Sarah Rowell (SR) started running seriously in 1981 and she has had three sets of physiological tests – in 1986 (aged 22, when in sub 2hr 30min marathon shape and having been training seriously for five years); 1998 (aged 34, when still competing seriously and in estimated sub 60min shape for 10 miles); and 2009 (aged

All ages can benefit from running drills. AUTHORS

47, focusing more on ultra events) – each with different but well-established physiologists who regularly work with top British athletes.

Normality might suggest that there would have been an increase in maximal oxygen uptake between tests one and two (as cumulative training age increased), followed by a decline at test three as less training and age set in, especially relative to weight, which went up by 2–3kg. Real life showed maximal oxygen uptake remaining the same across the 23-year period. What changed massively was running economy, which fell slightly between tests one and two (where, again, it might have been predicted to improve) and significantly between tests two and three, primarily due to loss of elasticity and optimal neural firing within the lower limbs. Put another way (and

using a car analogy), the engine and fuel delivery system was still great but the chassis was pretty worn out and needed replacing!

On a more practical note, from a training perspective in a situation like this, greater improvements (or more realistically, slower declines) in performance will most likely come about from incorporating appropriate functional exercises and drills into the training programme, compared with just doing more running.

Training Focus

From this we can see that there are different, but interlinked training adaptations that can all help improve running performance. What then are the best types of training to bring about these improvements? As runners we

Table 2: Different Types of Training and their Benefits

Training	Descriptor	Main Benefits	When Used	Examples
Easy	Pace at which you can easily hold a conversation	Recovery Use of lipids as fuel Local muscle strength and fatigability Cardiovascular adaptation	Easy/recovery runs Warm-up and warm-down before and after harder running	4–6 miles easy running
Steady	Pace at which you can talk but it is not easy	Cardiovascular adaptation Energy efficiency – both glycogen and lipid Running economy Local muscle strength and fatigability	Long runs Steady running	5–10 miles steady or 2–3hr long run
Sustained	Pace at or near the lactate threshold	Lactate threshold and tolerance Running economy Maximal oxygen uptake Neuro-muscular coordination	Threshold/sustained efforts. For races up to 60min in length this will also be near race speed	30min sustained run or 6 × 6min, 1min recovery or on hill
Race	Pace equating to the planned race speed	Operating at the predicted race speed and consequential physiological, mental and anatomical demands	Race pace – in most cases this is faster than steady running, but for ultra distances the opposite is often true	3–20 miles at predicted race pace (depending on planned race distance)
Speed	Pace is significantly faster than threshold – moving to sprinting	Leg speed Anaerobic capacity Peripheral movement Effectiveness and fatigue resistance Neuro-muscular coordination	Interval/Fartlek sessions – has potential to overlap with threshold running	10 × 400m, 200m jog or 10 × 80 sec, 80sec jog or on hills

use many terms to describe training – long runs, tempo, race pace, intervals, sustained, steady, easy, recovery, hard – words that mean something to us but may well mean something very different to someone else.

Table 2 gives a functional view of the different types of running training. While this is physiologically correct and reflects current thinking, it is a practical snapshot of something that in reality is more complicated and inter-related. It is an area that continues to generate debate and numerous scientific papers as scientists gradually increase their understanding of the body's underpinning physiology, biochemistry and neural adaptations to different training stimuli.

The terminology given is what will be used in the subsequent training-programme examples.

Of course, in real life things do not fall neatly into boxes, and in practice there is considerable overlap of training benefits across the different speeds/efforts of running. These in turn will alter depending on the length of the event being prepared for.

What does all this mean for the trail, mountain and fell runner? How do the various bits of information, sets of training principles and

Runners speed training in St Moritz. TRISS KENNY

types of training all fit together? What is the same as and what is different from running on the roads?

The answer to the latter question is two-fold: first, the runner needs to have the skills, experience and equipment to be safe when enjoying the freedom of running 'in the wilds' (these are covered in greater detail in Chapters 4 and 5). Second, running off-road adds another layer of complexity to training, one where there is greater emphasis on the terrain and topography of the event being prepared for. This is picked up in Chapter 2, before which we end this chapter with our ten guiding principles for training.

Guiding Principles for Training

These underpin the approach to training and are evident in all the training plans given in Chapter 2. They have been refined over the years through trial and error on our part as athletes and coaches and they take into account the different types of training and core training principles already mentioned. When followed, they provide a simple frame-work for the development of successful, individualized training programmes.

1. *Specific to You:* the individuality principle: everyone is different and training pro-grammes must be adapted to best fit individual genetics, training, biological age and personal circumstances. Two runners of the same age, having trained for the same length of time, doing the same amount of training each week, both with families and similar race times, will still benefit from customized training programmes. One runner, for example,

may be much better at running down-hill, while the other, due to weakened ankles but stronger hamstrings and gluteal muscles, better at running uphill. Their individual training focus needs to be different to optimize performance.

2. *The Long Run:* this should be a central and regular part of the training plan. There is no ideal length or running time for long runs, rather the optimal length depends on target race/event distance, the time in the training programme and individual runner profile.

3. *Keep Some Speed:* all effective training programmes must contain some sessions that are carried out at faster than predicted race pace; this will, in turn, help increase comfortable race-pace speed.

4. *Race Specific:* predicted race speed and distance must be trained for and prac-tised in training. Training at race pace for shorter distances, as well as separately building up to near-race distance, ideally over race-specific terrain, will help prepare you physiologically and mentally.

Even mountain-running greats like Marco de Casperi run easily sometimes. MARCO DE CASPERI

Even the amount of kit you need to wear is individual. DAN VERNON/NOVA INTERNATIONAL

5. *Terrain Specific:* training must take into account the terrain and topology of the targeted race, terrain underfoot, ascent and descent. It is no good doing lots of training on flat smooth surfaces if you want to race well and fast on undulating rocky paths.

6. *Recovery* – the hard/easy training principle: the most effective way to improve training and prevent underperformance is via a training programme with appropriate periods of recovery and rest built into it on a daily, weekly/monthly and annual basis. These are often referred to as microcycles, mesocycles and macrocycles.

7. *Prevention and Core:* a quality running programme should be supported by appropriate preventative proprioceptive and strengthening exercises to maximize performance. All runners will benefit from additional exercises to add strength, length or proprioceptive ability to soft tissues and joints.

8. *Race Craft:* this should be pre-planned and practised in training. Racing on trails and mountains adds additional dimensions to racing compared with the road, such as navigation, route choice, your and your opponents' ability over different types of terrain – all need to be factored into the race plan.

9. *Replacing Fuel and Fluid:* before, during and after training and racing, it is critical to optimize performance and recovery as well as prevent the body having greater susceptibility to illness or injury. There is no known magic food for runners, but getting your individual fuel and fluid intake right can make the difference between success and failure.

10. *Appropriate Kit and Equipment:* these

can make the difference between successfully completing a race or event and failing, let alone completing it well.

While all the above apply all the time, there is natural overlap or change in meaning depending on the nature of the event. In terms of pure 'running' training, it is principles 2–6 and how to manipulate them into a training programme that are focused on in Chapter 2. Principles 7–10 are looked at in more detail in later chapters.

CHAPTER 2

TAKING YOUR TRAINING OFF-ROAD

This is where it gets practical, looking at how the principles discussed in Chapter 1 translate into training programmes. First, however, it is worth giving consideration to how to run off-road.

How to Run Off-Road

To many this may seem obvious, but there are plenty of runners who struggle to adapt when switching from smooth tarmac to undulating, uneven trails. How, then, do you best adapt to the vagaries and variety encountered when running off-road?

On the road you can settle nicely into a rhythm, with an optimal stride length that is the same every time each foot hits the ground; off-road you must be prepared to chop and change to cope with the ever-changing nature of the terrain you are landing on. While this at times means overstriding, it is much better to shorten your stride so it becomes quicker and easier to react to the changes required, whether forward, left or right, to ensure your foot lands in the most suitable place while still maintaining speed and with as much stability as is possible.

Lengthening your stride should be avoided, not only as it means you are more unstable when you land, but also because increasing stride length so that you land with your foot too far in front of your body results in a braking action, hence slowing you down.

Shortening your stride, on the other hand, not only enables you to react quickly to the changes underfoot, but also to have a lighter and quicker foot-to-ground contact, ensuring that you maintain your speed as well as reduce the chances of injury due to falling or unstable foot plant.

The varied nature of trails and hence lack of rhythm when running means it is much harder to settle into a set pace or heart-rate zone and hold it for any length of time when off-road. Therefore, threshold or harder efforts should be judged more by perception, taking into account the nature of the terrain.

Runners who primarily run on road often complain that after running on trails their feet as well as some of the core stabilizing muscles and backside are sorer than they would be from a similar effort on smooth surfaces from having to work harder to cope with the changing terrain. Trail, mountain and fell runners, in turn, often find that their hamstrings and quadriceps cramp up when trying to run on flat smooth surfaces for significant periods. Here the consistent, rhythmic, repeatable running action that is required overloads the muscle in a way it is not used to, sending it into temporary cramp/spasm.

The other thing to focus on when running on trails is where you look. When running on roads it is often possible to look around, or to switch into a zone so that your eyes do not have to concentrate on what is coming up.

On trails there is a greater need to focus on the path in front of you, ideally looking two to three steps in front so that you anticipate and adapt in advance of the obstacles, be they rocks, roots or mud. This need to be able to see what is coming is why some runners, particularly off-road, find it difficult to run directly behind other runners without leaving a gap – they need more visual cues to ensure that they stay upright and uninjured. Running off-road regularly will help you get better at anticipation and slowly be able to look further ahead as you run, rather than directly at the ground in front of your feet.

Running on trails and mountains means running up and down hills. As with adapting from a smooth to an off-road surface, so changing from running on the flat to either up or down requires changes in body position and movement if you are to continue running smoothly and efficiently.

Running Uphill

All forms of trail, mountain and fell running involve at least some running uphill and, depending on the length and steepness of the climb(s), the uphill parts of a race are often where most time can be gained or lost. Making changes to your running stride, body position and deciding when to walk rather than run are all things to factor in with regard to how to get up the hill both as quickly as possible and, often more importantly, as efficiently as possible. The latter point is key because, other than uphill-only mountain races, few races finish at the top of the hill. In trail, fell and ultra races it is more common to have one or more hills en route. The ability, therefore, to keep running strongly when you reach the top of a hill becomes important. While not being the strongest of uphill runners, SR would frequently catch those who had passed her going uphill very soon after the top of the climb by running strongly

Working hard uphill with good technique. TRISS KENNY

off the hill while others ran slowly, recovering their breath from working (relatively) too hard on the climb.

For gentle inclines, particularly short ones, most runners will be able to run the whole of the uphill part. Assuming the hill is not just a short one up to the end of the race, then running uphill requires a different mindset from that of running hard during uphill reps (repetitions) or efforts. As above, both speed and efficiency of movement are important. One way of doing this is to aim to keep your perception of how hard you are working and/or your breathing rate the same, which of course means going slower (heart rate can also be used). As you switch into uphill mode, you should lean a little more into the hill and keep looking ahead of you, not just down at your feet, therefore remaining aware of any changes to terrain or obstacles. At the same time, shorten your stride, taking smaller, quicker steps and aiming to establish a good rhythm, which you can then keep going all the way to the top.

Smaller steps might at first seem a strange thing to do but, often, not only are they more efficient, they get you up the hill quicker. To find what works best for you, try doing a series of timed efforts at race pace up a 100m hill, changing your running stride from normal, to small steps and then striding out. In our experience, most runners find that shorter steps are more efficient and faster.

Finally, do not forget to use your arms: for short hills, a strong arm swing forward and back will help provide additional propulsion upwards; for longer ones, use your arms to help settle into a good rhythm (and do not worry if others shoot off fast at the start of the hill, you will probably catch them further up).

The steeper and the longer the uphill, the less 'runnable' it is, even for the elite runners. Deciding when to walk briskly uphill rather than run will come with experience but for each runner there is a point when continuing to run is less efficient than walking, both in terms of effort exerted and speed. Deciding when to walk can be gauged by the relative speed of other runners around you combined with your own perceived effort. Quite often, runners are influenced by those around them as well – if one starts to walk, so do those following.

When walking uphill hard, you should lean into the hill, thus lowering your centre of gravity; at the same time, use your arms to push down on your thighs, in effect using some upper body strength to 'drive' your legs. In fell races particularly, some steeper climbs mean it is often easier to climb for short periods on all fours, pulling yourself up using your hands, such as the final part of Whernside in the Three Peaks Race.

As with all aspects of running, practising in training is the best preparation for racing. It is sensible to start with 'bite-size' sections of uphill and gradually increase the length and steepness of the uphill sections and hence the time spent running upwards. For longer ultra races and mountain races, hillwalking with an emphasis on 'pushing' the uphill sections is an ideal way of training for uphill, and one used extensively by many top runners. If you can cope with many hours of hard hillwalking, then the uphill in trail, mountain and fell running becomes easy by comparison (see Chapter 10)!

- Start with short, gentle inclines, which are runnable.
- Gradually increase the duration of uphill running and also increase the gradient; as you progress, you will find the most comfortable angle to lean into the hill.
- As the duration increases, run for as long as possible and then change to brisk walking and practise pushing on your thighs and decide if this feels better and more comfortable for you (it does not suit everyone).
- Plan training sessions when you are going to concentrate on the uphill sections, using the other sections for recovery.
- Hill repetitions can be very useful training, when usually you will be moving faster than race pace, number and duration being dependent on race plans.
- If considering using poles for racing, their greatest value is probably when going uphill so this is an opportunity to familiarize yourself with their use (see Chapter 5).

Finally, remember that walking uphill is not a sign of weakness; rather, it is clever racing. It is not uncommon in steep uphill races to see those running being overtaken by others who are walking hard – finding what works best for you is the key.

Running Downhill

Whether running or racing on trails and mountains, being able to run downhill with confidence and a degree of control will not only add to your enjoyment but also make a big difference to how you perform. While running uphill is important, races can also be lost and won on the descent: it is more common for a trail or fell race to have a descent to the finish as opposed to an ascent. Being able to run fast downhill, particularly over rocky ground, is a great asset.

In order to run downhill well and often, there are two things runners need to prepare and train for. First, running downhill involves what is known as eccentric muscle contraction of the quadriceps muscles. Thinking back to Chapter 1, muscles are made up of numerous muscle fibres, and movement normally occurs by 'shortening' the muscle via the coupling and uncoupling

Good technique, descending at speed.
TRISS KENNY

of small cross bridges (think little hooks) between the fibres, pulling them across each other. Eccentric muscle contractions occur when the muscle lengthens under stress, so that it is acting to slow down and control the movement. When this occurs, there is thought to be damage to the cross bridges between the muscle fibres, the result of which, for the runner, is delayed onset muscle soreness (DOMS for short), whereby the affected muscles become very sore, tender to touch and have reduced power. In severe cases, this soreness can last for up to seven days.

The good news is that the more downhill running you do, the more your muscles become accustomed to it and the less sore they will be afterwards. Anyone planning on doing a race with long, steep or numerous descents should always include downhill running in their training, not only to get better at it, but to help ensure the muscle is conditioned to cope with the specific stresses.

The second area to consider is simply an ability to run downhill fast over what is often steep, uneven and unstable terrain. Runners who can descend well seem to skim over the surface, with their feet lightly and quickly acting to propel themselves downhill, with no break in movement. Those less well versed in the act of descending, stutter and slow down, landing more heavily and putting on a natural brake. While there are runners who are naturally good at running downhill, like all skills, anyone can get better with practice.

- When out on normal training runs, practise running downhill at speed, and as you build up confidence try ever steeper or rougher terrain.
- Do efforts that go both up and downhill (see the sections on training below).
- Watch (not while you are running) the techniques of good descenders and learn

from them – how they look ahead, use their arms for balance, often in a windmill-like action.
- Work out your preferred angle to lean, depending on the steepness of the hill – as a rule of thumb, the steeper the hill, the more you lean back and land on the mid-section or heel of your foot.
- Add proprioceptive drills to your training: starting on flat even ground, do drills designed to increase fast, quick movement. One way of doing this is to dot the ground with talcum powder and run quickly over the course, making sure your feet hit each of the dots, aiming to be light, quick and on your toes. As you become more confident, move the drills on to steeper and rougher ground and place the dots at more difficult angles/positions.
- Concentrate: running downhill fast over rough ground might require less effort physically, but it also needs maximum focus mentally (some might say the opposite to going uphill). It is often a loss of concentration that leads to falls.

Designing a Training Programme

Chapter 1 considered the things we need to take into account when designing a training programme; now it is time to get practical. Here there is value in reiterating that all training programmes should be individually designed to fit personal needs, limits and physiological, anatomical and psychological make-up and lifestyle.

A training programme should always be looked at as a moveable feast: something that starts off as an ideal, but which is adapted as you go along to take into account the twists and turns of everyday life – injury, family issues, work problems and so on. It is worth stressing that the best results come from consistency, but it is a very rare runner who never misses a day's training due to an injury niggle, illness or family/work issues. Much more important than missing the odd day or session is that the overall programme is a realistic one, which enables training to be consistently built on and progressed. The alternative – a series of unrealistic training spurts, intermixed by long periods of doing very little – achieves very little performance-wise and is unlikely to give much of a sense of achievement. Many runners when planning a training programme do so using miles or kilometres as the main training unit, with the training load measured in miles per week. While this has a lot of merit for those who run on the track or road, it has less value for trail, mountain and fell runners, where the conditions underfoot and steepness of the terrain will play a major part in how fast you can run and the potential training effect.

As an example, let us take 'Jim', a decent male runner whose best time for five miles is 30min. The path up Skiddaw in the Lake District is approximately four and a half miles with 931m of ascent. This takes Jim 50min running at the same level of effort as his five miles on the flat. Many trail, mountain and fell runners, therefore, use time as a training unit to give better recognition of the terrain covered.

Training Programme: Shape and Components

Most runners follow some sort of seven-day training schedule or routine, simply because that is the number of days in a week and hence gives a natural rhythm that fits with club training nights and weekends (the basic training cycle is often also referred to as a microcycle). There is, of course, no physiological or scientific reason why training programmes are based on seven days. Trying to fit all the key elements of training (long run,

hills, conditioning, threshold, race pace, speed work) into one week is near impossible while still allowing for appropriate recovery. In practice, many coaches look at covering all the elements by using a weekly pattern but alternating the 'harder' or key sessions over two to three weeks. The other alternative is to use an eight to ten day cycle, this being easier if you have flexible working arrangements. For ease of reference, in this book we will assume a weekly cycle is being used.

We are not aware of any scientific studies that have looked in-depth at this, but tradition, based on years of trial and error, leads most runners to doing three to four harder training sessions (including the long run) per week, with the other days a mixture of lower-intensity running, rest, cross-training or conditioning.

As well as balancing hard and easy training days within the weekly programme, runners need also to apply the same principle on a bigger scale: consciously planning blocks of harder and easier training to enable fitness to be built up to a peak prior to a key race or event, followed by an easier recovery period of training. Kenyan athletes are renowned not only for training very hard, but also for being able in their periods of recovery, or at the end of the racing season, to rest hard as well.

Again, there is no right or wrong way of doing this. Some runners mix hard weeks with easier ones, doing, for example, one or two hard training weeks (in terms of miles run and intensity of training) followed by an easier one. Other runners prefer a stepwise progression, gradually increasing the workload each week. Perhaps best is a mixture of the two, whereby the workload is slowly increased but there is a week of easier training every two to three weeks. The key, as ever, is finding out the approach that works best for you personally.

Example Training Programmes

This section provides an example of how the basic training programme format has been adapted to best prepare for each of the four specific races. The programmes all assume a strong base of running fitness and regular training; they are not designed as schedules for beginners and should be used in conjunction with the information in Chapter 7 on pre-race preparation. For all the examples:

- All effort sessions should be preceded and followed by a warm-up and warm-down.
- Experienced runners may want to add in some morning runs two to three times a week.
- Friday is a designated rest day, and must be treated as such, ideally as a non-running day, although some may prefer a short, very easy jog.

A 45min Fell Race

This is a typical British fell race, going to the top of a steep hill and back down, where there is off-path running, the race route is unmarked and runners can choose their own route.

> ### Key points:
>
> - The race will probably mean 30min of hard uphill effort followed by 15min of fast descending – this will mean working at or near your maximum heart rate for much of the period of climbing.
> - You need to balance the effort put into climbing with still being able to descend as fast as possible.

Learning from the Greats

Opposite is an example of a week's training programme from Ian Holmes. A multiple

Table 3: Sample Two-Week Training Programme for a 45-minute Fell Race

Monday	Steady 40–60min recovery run, ideally on undulating terrain, plus conditioning exercises
Tuesday	Speed work – 10–12 × 400m, 1min recovery on good flat surfaces/grass (or do 80sec efforts, 80sec recovery)
Wednesday	60min steady run on rough terrain, plus conditioning exercises
Thursday	45min run plus 10 × 1min uphill strides, with fast descent on grass
Friday	Rest/easy, jog/recovery, swim/bike
Saturday	Session of 2min hard, 1min recovery, 20min sustained, 1min recovery, 2min hard on a semi-rough surface requiring concentration on foot placement, etc.
Sunday	Long run – 90min, ideally on rough trails at a steady pace
Monday	Steady 40–60min recovery run, ideally on undulating terrain, plus conditioning exercises
Tuesday	Speed work, efforts of 1, 2, 3, 4, 3, 2, 1min, with 1min recovery – aiming to run faster over the shorter efforts, on a good surface, should feel hard but not flat out
Wednesday	60min run with faster pace 20min in the middle, plus conditioning exercises
Thursday	50min hilly rough fartlek, keeping the pace high on the descents – or just steady run if tired
Friday	Rest/easy, jog/recovery, swim/bike
Saturday	Hill efforts – 4 × 4min uphill, fast jog back down on a hill of similar steepness and underfoot conditions to the planned race (or ideally on the course itself)
Sunday	Long run – 75min on undulating trails at a steady to fast pace – talking is not easy

Table 4: Ian Holmes's One-Week Training Programme

	AM	PM	Notes
Monday	30min easy	50min easy	Won Scafell Pike the day before in 51.45
Tuesday	20min easy	Interval session – 3, 2, 2, 1 laps of cricket pitch	
Wednesday	20min easy	45min steady	
Thursday	20min easy	60min steady	
Friday	30min easy	Mini fartlek including 5 × 1-mile effort	
Saturday	Rest		
Sunday	Ian Hodgson relay 1st leg 73.06		

British and English fell-running champion, Ian has won most of the major fell races at some point in his career, from the very short to the ultralong such as Jura and Wasdale. It was

Ian Holmes. ANDY HOLDEN

over these races, lasting around 45min to an hour, that he was pretty much unbeatable in his prime. Here we include a typical training week from September 1993, towards the end of the season when Ian, a prolific racer, was still racing most weekends, but using lesser key races as hard training sessions.

A 90min Mountain Race
This is a traditional uphill European mountain race.

> **Key points:**
>
> - It is not dissimilar in physiological requirement to that of a half marathon, it requires you to be running at or near your threshold workload for the whole race.
> - If in Europe, altitude may become an issue, as could heat (see Chapter 4).
> - Cycling is excellent for developing the muscles used for climbing (this is covered further in Chapter 3).

Learning from the Greats
Overleaf is an example week's training from Jonathan Wyatt, six times world mountain running champion and widely considered to

Table 5: Sample Two-Week Training Programme for a 90-minute Mountain Race

Monday	Steady 40–60min recovery run, ideally on undulating terrain, plus conditioning exercises
Tuesday	Speed work – 4–8 × 800m, 2min recovery on flat good surfaces/grass (or efforts of 2min 30sec)
Wednesday	90–120min bike ride, plus conditioning exercises
Thursday	Fast relaxed hill session – 8–12 × 60sec uphill, focusing on good form, driving with arms and legs (if tired, then 50min steady run plus a few strides at the end or 60–90min bike ride)
Friday	Rest/easy, jog/recovery, swim/bike
Saturday	30min sustained/race pace effort, if possible done uphill (or equivalent on bike or stepper)
Sunday	Long run – 2hr ideally, on undulating trails at a steady pace or up to 4hr on the bike
Monday	Steady 60–90min bike ride* run, ideally on undulating terrain, plus conditioning exercises
Tuesday	Speed work – 4–5 sets of 120sec, 90sec, 45sec, 45sec recovery, 2min between sets on flat good surfaces/grass
Wednesday	Steady to sustained pace 60min run, plus conditioning exercises
Thursday	50–60min run or bike/stepper equivalent, including 10 × 45sec hard, 45sec easy, ideally on trails
Friday	Rest/easy, jog/recovery, swim/bike
Saturday	Hill efforts (or equivalent on the bike/step machine) – 5 × 5min uphill, 2min quick jog back (on a long hill this means you can gradually work your way up the hill)
Sunday	Long run – 90min on undulating trails at a steady to fast pace – talking is not easy

* Aim for two to three sessions on the bike a week – mix and match both steady sessions and hard ones as well.

Table 6: Jonathan Wyatt's One-Week Training Programme

	AM	PM	Notes
Monday	Easy 1hr run		Travel day
Tuesday	Hill session	Gym or rest	Unless the race was a long one, in which case I make adjustments with Tuesday an easy run of 1hr 30min
Wednesday	Easy 1hr 45min–2hr 15min run	Rest	
Thursday	Steady long uphill run about 1hr 30min–2hr	Easy road bike 2hr	
Friday	Easy undulating 1hr 30min run	Walk/jog with dog	
Saturday	Easy 1hr run		Travel day
Sunday	Race		

be the world's greatest mountain runner, particularly in uphill races.

Training revolves around two harder workouts per week (Tuesday and Thursday) and one long run. Sometimes if the race is not too tough; he uses that as a workout too and puts the long run on Monday.

Typical sessions:

- 8 × 3min on a fairly steep but runable uphill with 2min recovery.
- 10 × 60sec, more like hill fartlek.
- Long, steady climb, if possible 20–30min (often this will be also the long run).

A 3hr Trail Race

This race is on a mix of undulating trails, grasslands, paths, bits of roads; the race checkpoints must be visited, but may be marked; some support en route provided.

Key points:

- It is not dissimilar in physiological requirement to that of a marathon.
- Consider adding extra training, without added impact, via one or two sessions on the bike a week.

Learning from the Greats

While we would hesitate to use the label 'Greats' to describe us, for the 3hr trail race we give examples of our training from spring 1991. At the time, we were both running well and both focusing on two long trail/fell races: the Haworth Hobble (33 miles done in pairs) and the Yorkshire Three Peaks (24 miles of decent running, often likened to a marathon, with three hills along the way). That year we broke the women's record at the Hobble, running 4hr 38min, and then both ran well at the Three Peaks, where SR broke the

Jonathan Wyatt. MATTHIAS ROBI

Table 7: Sample Two-Week Training Programme for a 3-hour Trail Race

Monday	Steady 60min recovery run, ideally on undulating terrain, plus conditioning exercises
Tuesday	Speed work 5–6 × 6min, 2min recovery on flat good surfaces/grass
Wednesday	60–90min steady on undulating surfaces, plus conditioning exercises
Thursday	60min on a hilly undulating course – including 12 × 45sec fast relaxed, 45sec float recovery (see p.40)
Friday	Rest/easy, jog/recovery, swim/bike
Saturday	60–70min sustained/race pace effort or shorter race
Sunday	Long run – 2.5hr ideally on undulating trails at a steady pace
Monday	Steady 50min plus conditioning exercises
Tuesday	Speed work – 4 × 3min, 90sec recovery, 90sec, 90sec recovery on flat good surfaces/grass – feeling should be fast but not flat out
Wednesday	60min run, including three 5-min race pace efforts in the middle, plus conditioning exercises
Thursday	Fast relaxed hill session – 12–16 × 60sec uphill plus10m over the top, focusing on good form, driving with arms and legs, 2–3 miles warm-up and warm-down
Friday	Rest/easy, jog/recovery, swim/bike
Saturday	On undulating trails – 20min sustained, 3min recovery, 6–8 × 80sec fast relaxed, 80sec float
Sunday	Long run – 2hr on undulating trails at a steady to fast pace – talking is not easy, followed straight away by 30min on the turbo trainer/bike

women's record by over 15min, winning in 3hr 16min, while WD ran her fastest-ever time of 3hr 37min.

Table 8 shows the final hard eight days three weeks before the Three Peaks and, three weeks after, the Hobble.

Table 8: Sarah Rowell's Eight-Day Training Programme

	AM	PM	Notes
Sunday	2hr 20min undulating terrain (19 miles)		Talking difficult
Monday	5 miles steady		
Tuesday	6 miles steady	Interval session 6 × 3min on grass	Feeling good
Wednesday	9 miles along canal	4 miles easy	
Thursday	5 miles	6 miles inc. 16 × 45sec on:off	Feeling tired, legs heavy
Friday	6 miles steady		
Saturday	Wardle Skyline Race – 7 miles, 1st in 46.17, men's winner 41.26		
Sunday	24-mile recce of Three Peaks with WD, out about 4.5hr		

Table 9: Wendy Dodds' Eight-Day Training Programme

Same week as for SR – WD's approach was more racing and easier training during the week.

	AM	PM	Notes
Sunday	Kentmere Horseshoe Race 1hr 54min		
Monday	45min easy		
Tuesday	75min steady		
Wednesday	60min steady		
Thursday	Rest		
Friday	35min easy		
Saturday	Wardle Skyline Race – 7 miles, 52.42		
Sunday	24-mile recce of Three Peaks with SR, out about 4.5hr		

A young Sarah Rowell winning the Three Peaks in 1999 (left), and an older Wendy Dodds winning age-group category, Turner landscape, 2012. DAVE WOODHEAD (left) and IAN CHARTERS

A 10-Hour Plus Ultra Race

On a mix of undulating trails/grasslands, paths, roads; the race route must be followed but it is not marked; some support en route provided at the checkpoints.

> **Key points:**
>
> - Race pace will most likely be slower than normal steady training pace and should be practised in training.
> - A race of this length, while still very physiologically demanding, requires great mental strength – it is often about who can mentally handle the distance and 'bad' patches the best.
> - Time on your feet in training becomes important; think also about adding biking to your training to increase the workload but without the loading stress on the body.
> - If in Europe, altitude and heat may become an issue (see Chapter 4)

Learning from the Greats

Jez Bragg is one of the world's top distance runners whether on the trails or the roads, with perhaps winning the 2010 Ultra Trail du Mont Blanc his greatest achievement, and winning Commonwealth gold in 2009 in the 100km road race close behind. His performances over shorter ultra races are of a similar quality and in 2010 he broke the long-standing record for the Fellsman among others. Here he talks us through his training:

My training philosophy is very much based around trying to 'tune in' to how my body is feeling and to train accordingly, rather than force it into doing something it's not ready for during any one session. I think this is particularly important for high mileage runners in peak training, who will inevitably be treading the fine line between pushing it hard to improve fitness and simply over-doing it. This approach has generally been very successful for me in avoiding over-

Table 10: Sample Two-Week Training Programme for a 10-hour Plus Ultra Race

Monday	60–80min recovery run, plus conditioning exercises
Tuesday	Speed work – 8–10 × 800m, 2min recovery, on flat good surfaces/grass, fast relaxed at threshold pace (or do 2min 30sec efforts)
Wednesday	90–120min steady, plus conditioning exercises
Thursday	75min steady/easy, inc. 12 × 45sec fast relaxed
Friday	Rest/easy, jog/recovery, swim/bike
Saturday	90min–2hr run at faster than planned race pace, or local race of similar length
Sunday	Long run – 4hr, aiming for planned race pace, ideally over part of the race route or similar terrain
Monday	Easy 60min run, ideally on undulating terrain, plus conditioning exercises
Tuesday	Sustained session – 3–4 × 10min sustained, 2min recovery on undulating paths
Wednesday	Steady to decent pace 60min run, plus conditioning exercises
Thursday	75min steady, inc. 8 × 1min fast relaxed uphill
Friday	Rest/easy, jog/recovery, swim/bike
Saturday	60min fartlek session plus warm-up and warm-down, optional additional 2hr on the bike
Sunday	Long walk/jog in the hills 6–8hr

training. It effectively means training to a weekly structure with a degree of fluidity to it, rather than anything too rigid.

In other words, I know all the sessions that I want to fit in each week, but I will be flexible about when I run them, depending upon how I am feeling. I will tend to run the hard and fast sessions such as intervals, tempo runs or hill reps when I feel fresh and strong, but ease back for recovery runs when I'm feeling tired or at all run down. Quite often I won't decide exactly what the session will entail until I get running and I'm properly warmed up.

A peak training week for a long ultra such as the Fellsman or Western States 100 is shown in Table 11.

Jez Bragg. THE NORTH FACE.

Table 11: Long Ultra One-Week Training Programme

	AM	PM	Notes
Monday	Rest	10 miles easy/recovery*	
Tuesday	5 miles steady*	7 miles tempo*	Tempo can vary from 7 to 10 miles
Wednesday	Rest	15 miles steady	Midweek 'medium' run on the hills with a friend
Thursday	5 miles easy	Hill reps or intervals. e.g. 6 × 1 mile	Easy runs sometimes substituted with a swim or cycle ride (road)
Friday	5 miles easy	7 miles easy	
Saturday	Long trail run replicating the race terrain/conditions – 25–40 miles with 50 per cent at race pace	–	Choosing an interesting/purposeful route, e.g. Poole to Weymouth along the coast path or a loop in the Purbeck Hills
Sunday	12–15 miles steady	Walk/swim/gym	Sometimes the Saturday/Sunday runs will be back-to-back 'medium' length runs of c.20 miles.

* Easy/recovery runs: 7.00–8.00min/mile

* Steady runs: 6.30–7.00min/mile

* Tempo runs: 5.45–6.00min/mile

Ideas to Try

The options for training-programme design are limited only by our imagination. Below are ideas that we have used in training for specific purposes and can be easily adapted to fit any of the training programmes above to add some variety.

1. *20:20* – a session concept, which gives great variety. When run hard it is a great way of improving lactate threshold via a series of fast surges while running at speed. It involves running for a period of time (10–30min, or blocks of 10–15min) repeating bouts of 20sec hard, 20sec fast float (namely, keeping running at a steady, comfortable pace). When done at a hard pace, heart rate will stay high throughout as the body also gets better at adapting to regular surges in speed while running fast.

    The 'hardness' of the session can, however, easily be adapted by changing the speed of the fast or slower bouts. This makes it a great session to use to reintroduce faster running when first getting back into training after a rest period or break due to injury. Here the focus is on 'fast relaxed' running rather than 'fast sustained' or 'fast pushing it'.

2. *Repeated climbs* – some races require you to climb, descend and then very quickly climb again. Being able to climb hard straight after a fast descent is a skill in itself and one worth practising in training if you know that's what the race will require.

    Example session: 3–4 efforts of 2–3min climb, fast descent (this will also help condition your legs for descending) and straight into another 2–3min climb; 3min recovery between efforts.

This concept was used successfully by Jonathan Wyatt, who used the session to improve his ability to climb again after descending hard, helping him win the up and down World Championships in 2005.

A variation on this is used by the Italian mountain runners, using a 3km circuit with 1km climb, 1km descent and 1km flat, done as sustained efforts.

3. *Learning to run tired (1)* – being successful at racing, particularly longer races, means being able to cope physically and mentally with running hard when you feel tired. Something not to be approached lightly but which, if done carefully, can be very effective is the East German idea of double hard days, where you train hard two days running, meaning on the second day you are literally running tired.

    Example session: if training for a 90min mountain race, do a speed-based interval session on the Tuesday, followed on the Wednesday by a 90min run, 60min of which are at threshold/race pace.

4. *Learning to run tired (2)* – on a similar note, one of the conundrums of training for long races (over three hours) is the balance between doing runs of a similar length in training versus the increased risk of injury or overtiredness. One way around this is to do a long run in the morning, 2–2.5hr, and then do a hard 30min run in the afternoon – or even a short race. This gets you used to running hard on tired legs both physically and mentally.

5. *Adding to your long runs* – another solution to the same problem, especially if training for a race that has a number of longish climbs in it is to do a long run (2–3hr) and then jump straight on the

bike or turbo trainer for 30–40min. Again, you are having to work hard physically and mentally on tired legs but this time without the physical impact stress of running. Cycling is also great training for running uphill.

6. *Over the top* – slightly similar to the repeated climbs concept, in races the effort does not stop at the top of the hill. Even in uphill-only races, there is often a flat run to the finish. Being good at climbing is of little use if you cannot then sustain your effort over the top and the runners you previously passed now shoot back past you as you recover.

Example session: do efforts using a hill that allows you to run hard on the flat for 30–50m after the climb; the number of efforts is dependent upon the time taken.

7. *Ethiopian fartlek* – named after its apparent originators, this is a slightly different take on normal fartlek, adapting it to off-road running. The aim is to improve your ability to run fast over undulating, mixed underfoot terrain. As you improve, you should find that you are able to maintain your running speed at all times. Likewise, your heart rate and feeling of effort should reflect that of a sustained pace session.

Example session: using an area of mixed, undulating, off-road terrain, after warming up, do 20–40min worth of effort whereby flat and uphill sections are run at a sustained pace, with the descents taken as a fast float for recovery; there is no jogging or easy running during the effort time.

8. *The end/start sprint* – it is not unusual for some trail, mountain and fell running races to be quite narrow at the start,

plus of course there are always times when a good sprint finish is required to outkick the opposition.

Example session: add 3–5 × 45sec sprints (45sec recovery) to the start or end of a sustained run. The session therefore becomes 5 × 45sec (45sec recovery), followed straight away by 20–30min sustained running.

9. *Mid-race surges* – all runners can do with having to put in a mid-race surge: picking up the pace for a short while before settling back to your racing speed. The key is being able to do so without having to slow down below race speed after the surge. How often do you see people in races making a big effort to get past someone, only to then slow right down and get re-over-taken – all that effort for nothing? In trail, mountain and fell races, not only might you want to surge to get away from someone, but also to take advantage of narrow parts of the course, where overtaking is difficult. It's important to be able to accelerate quickly to the front of a group to avoid being caught behind slower runners.

Example session: during a long run or race pace effort, add a number of faster surges, lasting between 30sec and 4min, aiming to maintain your pace when not surging and not slow to a jog recovery. Better still, get a friend or coach with you to blow a whistle to start and stop surges so you do not know how long they will last. This is not an easy session; make sure you have enough recovery before and after.

10. *Kenyan hills* – hills tend to be run as efforts; go hard and then jog-down recovery. The alternative is to combine hills and sustained running, as the Kenyans are often said to do, resulting

in a session that not only is a great way of boosting cardiovascular fitness (maximal oxygen uptake), but also enhancing hill running ability, leg power, running economy and conditioning your legs for running downhill.

Example session: after warming up, on a looped course with one to three climbs of 2–5min each, run continuously at a sustained pace for 20–40min (build up to 40min). When done correctly, this is a hard session during which your heart rate will stay in the threshold zone all the time.

11. *Fat metabolism* – something to be treated with a degree of caution as it will feel hard. As noted in Chapter 1, a key adaptation for being a good long-distance runner is your ability to get a greater percentage of your energy from fat metabolism compared with carbohydrate. One way of training your body to do this is to run for longer distances (90–120min) first thing in the morning without eating. This means your circulating blood sugar levels are low, forcing your body to become better at using fat. Adaptation takes 6–8 weeks on average and requires persistence. It is important to drink during the longer runs but only water, or water with electrolytes. Using drinks with calories defeats the object. As you increase the length of your runs, you can still use the 'train on empty' technique and you will find the duration you can comfortably go on for increases. The other way is to stay empty for the first two hours and then eat or drink carbohydrate as normal (for example, about 60g per hour).

Hills

Hills are key for trail, mountain and fell runners because not only are they a great way of improving running performances per se and are frequently used by runners of all standards and distances from 200m upwards as part of their training, but being able to run well up and down hills is a key component of enjoying and competing in most trail and certainly any mountain or fell race.

The limit to using hills in training is only one of the mind. Hills can be used in a variety of ways depending on the training effect wanted:

- *Endurance* – incorporate hills into threshold or sustained runs (see the sections on Kenyan hills and Ethiopian fartlek above).
- *Strength endurance* – do longer reps of 3–5min with short recovery (1min) on a medium gradient hill.
- *Strength* – using a medium to steep hill, drive up it hard for 30–40sec, jog down and repeat 10–20 times.
- *Power* – using a steeper, short hill, bound up the slope for 10–15sec, focusing on good running technique with a powerful arm and leg drive and quick, fast foot contact with the ground; walk back recovery and repeat 6–12 times.
- *Running form* – as above, but for 30–40sec on a slightly less steep hill, still driving with the arms and legs but less of a bounding action (this is less about how fast you get up the hill, more about doing so with good form); jog back recovery and repeat 12–25 times.
- *Broken rhythm* – running up on rocky paths where the focus is on moving quickly and lightly over the rocks, tree roots and so on, building up speed and confidence while your running stride is

continually having to chop and change to cope with the ever-changing, uneven and often unstable surfaces.

Using trekking poles with an aggressive arm action when running uphill has long been utilized by runners to get a whole body workout and can be of benefit whether you plan to race with poles or not.

In preparation for racing, it is useful to find a local hill with a similar 'profile' to the hills in the event, making the hill training more specific for the competition. Here you should run both up and down the hill hard, as you would in the race. Some will use longer/steeper hills so that when fatigued during a race, the event hills are more 'manageable'.

CHAPTER 3

SUPPLEMENTARY TRAINING

If you want to be a better runner, the most important thing to do is run; for the most part, this is true. Specific running training is the most important element required to bring about improved running performance and, for many years, the coaching creed was: 'running is key and all that is required'.

Current consensus is now that, while running is key to being a better runner, there are significant gains to be had from supplementing this with other forms of training, not only to help improve running performance, but also to help minimize the risk of physical injury and/or physical or psychological staleness.

In particular, supplementary training can help in a number of ways:

- It can provide a physiological training stimulus without the physical loading of running. Elite runners frequently supplement their running with less impactful forms of aerobic exercise such as running in water or on an anti-gravity treadmill, cycling, cross-country skiing, elliptical trainer (a machine requiring a lower limb movement, which is a cross between running and cross-country skiing and may or may not also involve arm movement) and swimming.

- It can provide an alternative form of exercise during end of season breaks, enabling you to continue to enjoy the benefits of exercise, while at the same time giving your body a well-deserved rest from running.

- The action of running does a great job at strengthening and improving the soft tissues and body systems that are directly involved in the activity, such as the major muscles in the legs. There are other closely associated muscles, for example the minimus and medius gluteal muscles, which, if weak, have the potential to affect running performance adversely in a serious way and/or increase injury risk. These are best strengthened via targeted exercises designed to both strengthen and engage the muscles, so that they do their job optimally when you run.

- Likewise, there are what could be called secondary areas, such as the trunk and shoulders, where a certain level of all-round strength and tone can help optimize running performance (especially if you plan to do a lot of running wearing a rucksack). This again is best gained from additional specific exercises, particularly if you have a sedentary job. Those who on a day-to-day basis carry out more active work, may well find that they develop these areas naturally.

- It can help you prepare to race or run on surfaces not available on your doorstep; in particular, making use of cycling, stairs, or similar, for races involving a lot of ascending, or using wobble cushions and similar, to mimic and hence prepare better for running on unstable surfaces.

This chapter looks in more detail at training modalities that trail, mountain and fell runners can use to supplement or complement their running training. Later in the book, Chapter 10 covers cross-training in more detail; in other words, the types of training that can be carried out as alternatives to running.

In practice, there is significant crossover between the concepts of supplementary and cross-training and what forms of exercise fall into each. Between the two they provide an array of different ways in which you can support and enhance your running-specific training.

Strength

Why Strength Training?

If endurance relates to the ability to keep going for a long time, strength is about how strong something is. Although absolute strength is not vital for running, having a well-rounded level of all-over body strength is now recognized as important for successful endurance performance and it is an unusual elite endurance runner, whatever the surface, who does no supplementary strength training.

Key benefits of strength training for trail, mountain and fell runners are:

- Strong muscles around a joint will help minimize injury if there is unexpected movement not in the direction of travel, something particularly pertinent when running on unstable and ever-changing surfaces – strong ankles are key to being able to enjoy and perform well on rougher off-road surfaces.
- Upper body strength is important for uphill running in a number of ways. Having a strong arm drive provides added momentum when running up and over shorter hills; on longer runnable climbs, a decent and consistent arm swing helps you maintain a steady rhythm; on steeper

walking climbs you can use your arms to push down on your thighs, helping drive uphill movement, while on very steep climbs arms may be used on the ground to 'pull' you up the hill. Likewise, if you are using poles (see Chapter 5), which can transfer up to 25 per cent of body weight to the arms, then upper body strength is an advantage – indeed, it is not unknown for runners using poles for the first time to find that it is their arms that tire the quickest due not being used as much previously.

These are in addition to the benefits of strength training for all runners:

- To increase running speed, you have to do one of two things (or a combination of both): increase your stride length (the amount of ground you cover per stride) or increase your stride turnover (how quickly your legs go round, including the time spent on ground contact) and be able to do this without one adversely affecting the other. (If you try to increase your stride length too much you often end up overstriding, which has a natural braking effect, therefore slowing down stride turnover.) Stronger muscles (and associated soft tissues) will potentially enable you to both generate more force and therefore increase stride length as well as stride frequency due to a quicker and more forceful ground contact phase. Strength will also help ensure you become tired less quickly, therefore maintaining stride frequency and length.
- In accordance with the overload training principle mentioned in Chapter 1, the muscles involved in running will adapt to the stress placed on them, developing to become strong enough to cope with the load placed on them. To develop a

stronger and more powerful muscle, you need to overload it above and beyond this, and one way of doing this is via appropriate strength-based exercises. Once the muscle is stronger, this in theory can then be translated into a more powerful running action (a longer stride), which can be maintained for longer at a particular pace (stride turnover).

- Running leads to the muscles being used getting stronger; it does not have the same effect on the opposing muscles, which do not get so much use, or on those with the primary role of more as a stabilizer than a mover. These, at best, become less strong, at worse weaker. Strength exercises to counteract this potential imbalance are important – for example, exercises for the gluteal muscles.

Strength Training for Runners

As opposed to applying a light load for prolonged periods to improve endurance, strength is improved by moving a heavier load. Measuring strength or setting training programmes is often referred to in terms of an individual's one repetition maximum (1RM) (the heaviest load/weight that can be lifted once only), or similarly 5RM, 10RM and so on.

Important leg muscle groups for runners to consider for strengthening are: hamstrings, quadriceps, calves, while not forgetting the adductors and abductors (the latter are important to help stabilize the pelvis during running). While this is more critical in road running, where the forces going through the pelvis are equal on both sides and repetitive, it is also key for successful trail, mountain and fell running. In addition, runners should consider including some whole-body exercises, which strengthen the upper body and trunk, into their training.

Power is different from strength in that it brings in speed; it is essentially the rate of doing work, and exercises to improve this reflect the speed element. For example, if a measure of pure strength is how much you can lift in one go, a measure of power would include how quickly the weight can be lifted or applied (as in running fast uphill). In applied sporting terms, it is normally power that is more important than pure strength; however, base strength is needed to be converted into power.

Strength training for trail, mountain and fell running does not mean that you have to go to the gym and start lifting weights. While this is one option, most runners can get just as an effective strength workout using their own body weight plus a few small pieces of home-based equipment; the key is doing so in a manner that places a greater load on a particular muscle compared with what would occur during running. Those runners wanting a gym-based programme, whether using free weights or machines to complement their running, are best advised to seek the advice of a gym professional, who should also be able to help you with your exercise choice and technique.

Key Strength-Training Guidelines

Before looking at the exercises in detail, it is worth noting the key guidelines to keep in mind when adding strength-based work to your training regime.

- *Why?* – you should always be very clear why you are doing a certain exercise, on which muscles it is designed to impact and how (strengthen/make more powerful/increase proprioceptive ability).
- *How much?* – always remember you are using strength training to complement your running, it is not about becoming as strong as possible, but rather getting the

strength you need to make you a better runner.

- *How often?* – linked to the above, most runners will find that one or two strength-based sessions a week of no more than 45min will be enough. It is possible to maintain strength levels with one focused 30–45min strength session a week. Many runners, therefore, do two sessions during the winter season, dropping this to one when they are racing more in the summer.
- *When?* – how best to fit your strength sessions into the training week? Commonly, runners will do them on days when they are doing less intense running. However, if you are just starting out on a strength programme, some exercises (lunges, for example) are likely to leave you feeling sore the next day, so think about when it is best to fit them into your schedule.
- *Technique* – making sure you have the correct technique for any strength or rehabilitative exercise is key. Poor or wrong technique will at best develop the wrong muscles and hence be ineffective in helping you as a runner; at worse, will increase injury risk. It is much better to do exercises with a slightly lower weight and perfect technique as opposed to a bigger weight and poor technique. A short anecdote about SR is relevant here: she had very weak gluteal muscles, but was able to do most of the exercises set by physiotherapists designed to theoretically strengthen them by engaging her back or hamstring muscles. She was therefore happily doing the exercises thinking she was correcting a key weakness, but with no impact – it took a very controlled and careful exercise programme to isolate the gluteal muscles in a way they could be strengthened.

- *Safety* – particularly key if using free weights, always ensure you train in a safe and appropriate environment.
- *Reps and sets* – the issue of the optimal number of reps (repetitions in one go), sets (the number of times you carry out the reps in a session) and the recovery time between them, is one which continues to be debated by strength professionals. For the purposes of general strength improvement/maintenance for trail, mountain and fell runners, doing 2–3 sets of between 6–15 reps is ideal.

Functional Stability

Core stability has become a buzzword of late, with whole books and exercise regimes based around improving your 'core', or as is normally referred to, 'core stability'. Core stability generally refers to the strength of the core, namely the trunk. For runners it is better to focus more on functional stability, which includes not only the core, but also the way in which the body moves as a whole, including the muscles around the pelvis, the way the arms and legs move on the trunk, and includes posture during movement. The reason that these muscle groups are important in trail, mountain and fell running is that body position, and hence posture, is continually changing and the better the control that you have over this, the more fluent and efficient will be your running style.

Having good functional stability will therefore help ensure that not only is your running style optimal, but it stays that way in the latter stages of a run when you are tired. If your core is weak, then the chances are that your stride will become more inefficient as you tire, leading to slower times and/or increased injury potential. This inefficiency is due to an increased tendency in those with poor functional stability to brace with all of their muscles to gain control, in turn resulting in becoming too rigid, rather than being controlled, fluid and efficient. This is something that can also result in a poor breathing pattern, which further affects performance.

If your pelvis is likened to a platform that you want to keep stable, then as a trail, mountain and fell runner it is also important to have stability in both the other major body platforms: the ankles and – albeit to a lesser extent – the shoulders.

Conditioning Exercises for Trail, Mountain and Fell Runners

Given below are key exercises for trail, mountain and fell runners that the authors use as part of their complementary training programmes and as recommended by the Coach House Sports Physiotherapy Clinic. They are ones chosen specifically to enhance muscle strength as well as functional stability and are relevant for trail, mountain and fell runners. While some people separate strength exercises from functional ones, for most runners it is more time efficient as well as easier to combine the two into one compact exercise session (and more enjoyable, too).

There are plenty of alternative exercises that are used by and recommended for runners, and part of the fun is mixing and matching exercises to avoid staleness and keep the training stimulus fresh (remember the training principle of progression: once the body has reached a certain fitness level, to progress you have to change or increase the physical stimulus) – the key is always referring back to the guidelines of why? And how much? And, where necessary, getting the advice from a coach or physiotherapist to keep you progressing in the right direction

and ensuring that what you do will help your running.

Theraband is a rubber material that can be used as resistance for strengthening exercises. It comes in a variety of colours, each one requiring a different amount of effort to work against the resistance offered by the rubber. By working against this resistance almost every muscle group can be strengthened. It has the advantage of being light and portable and ideal for use at home.

The Key Trail, Mountain and Fell Runner's Conditioning Circuit

1. Quadriceps Stretch
- Lie on your side, bottom knee bent up level with hips.
- Tighten abdominals and flatten back.

Quadriceps stretch. COACH HOUSE PHYSIOTHERAPY CLINIC

- Hold top ankle so that the heel is touching your buttock.
- Pull top leg back behind you until good stretch is felt in front of thigh.
- Keep knee lower than hip and back flat.
- Hold 30sec × 3.

2. Hamstring Stretch

- Sit on chair.
- Perfect posture, with good lumbar arch (lordosis).
- Slowly straighten one leg, maintaining perfect posture.

Soleus raise. *COACH HOUSE PHYSIOTHERAPY CLINIC*

Hamstring stretch. *COACH HOUSE PHYSIOTHERAPY CLINIC*

- Full stretch is the point just before the back starts to lose its lordosis.
- Hold 30sec × 5.

3. Calf Stretch and Strengthen

3A SOLEUS RAISES (DEEP CALF)
- Stand facing the wall, on one leg with the knee bent.

- Keep knee over second toe at all times.
- Without moving hips, lift heel off floor and go on to toes, then lower.
- Do not let knee fall in.
- Go through full range, aiming for smooth movement.
- Build up to 3 × 25 repititions (reps).
- Do daily after running.

3B GASTROCNEMIUS RAISES (STRAIGHT KNEE)
- Stand on edge of step on one leg with knee straight.
- Fingers on wall for balance.
- Go up and down with heel, keeping knee straight.
- Go through full range with a smooth movement.
- Build up to 3 × 25 reps.

Gastrocnemius raise. COACH HOUSE PHYSIOTHERAPY CLINIC

- Do daily after running.
  (Once this becomes easy, you can make it more plyometric on alternate days by going for speed upwards.)

4. Glute Engagement

- Lie on your side, with your hips at 45 degrees and knees at 90 degrees.
- Keeping your feet together, use your top leg glut muscles to slowly lift your top knee up and down repetitively – it looks like you are imitating a clam opening and closing.
- Key here is that you lead the movements with the leg and do not rotate your pelvis backwards or shorten at your waist/hitch the hip to get the range of movement needed.
- Build up to 2 sets of 30sec each side.

PROGRESSION
- Straighten your top leg in line with your body.
- Keeping your top leg and knee straight,

Glute engagement. COACH HOUSE PHYSIOTHERAPY CLINIC

turn your leg out, pointing your toes toward the ceiling.

- Raise and lower your leg slowly to hip height and down, keeping the leg just behind your hip.
- Do 2–3 sets of 30sec; do not allow the leg to drift forward.

5. Thoracic Rotation

This exercise ensures your upper and lower back are moving freely, aiding balance, technique and breathing.

- Sit with a relaxed posture, hands on lap.
- Keep head still, and rotate through lower ribcage.
- Your shoulders will move as your ribs move, they shouldn't be pulling you into rotation.
- Do × 20 little and often and for warm-up.

Functional balance. COACH HOUSE PHYSIOTHERAPY CLINIC

6. Functional Balance

- Stand on one leg and turn your head from side to side, saying the days of the week out loud.
- Make sure you do not screw up your toes.
- By turning your head, speaking and breathing, you are training your balance reactions without using non-functional bracing strategies.

7. Functional Dynamic Balance

- Stand on one leg on a small step so that your other leg is hanging over the space.

Thoracic rotation. COACH HOUSE PHYSIOTHERAPY CLINIC

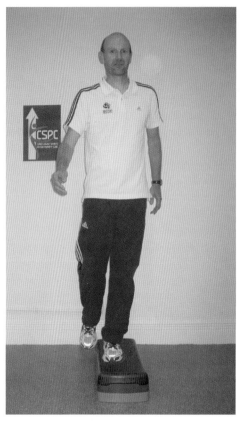

Functional dynamic balance. COACH HOUSE PHYSIOTHERAPY CLINIC

- Make sure your pelvis is level, swing your arms and non-standing leg as if you were walking.
- The exercise should feel easy and can be progressed to incorporate 'running arms and leg'.
- Take care not to curl or grip with the toes of your standing leg.
- 3–4 sets of 15–30sec depending on level of difficulty.

8. Bird Dog

This exercise is for spinal stability.

- On hands and knees, hands under shoulders, knees directly under hips, hips at 90 degrees, elbows slightly bent.
- Your back should be in a perfect posture, parallel with the floor – move your hands forward if necessary and keep your neck lengthened.
- Slowly lift your opposite hand and knee, aiming to maintain spinal alignment at all times.
- Straighten out the lifted arm and leg until your elbow and knee are both straight, reaching out through your fingertips and heel, aiming to get your thigh and arm parallel to the ground.

Bird dog. COACH HOUSE PHYSIOTHERAPY CLINIC

- Return to start, keeping your heel at 90 degrees.
- Do not let your pelvis tilt; maintain your spinal alignment.
- Repeat × 10 each leg – 3 sets.

9. Lunges

9A STATIC LUNGES

- Stand with one foot in front of the other, pelvis straight, good posture.
- Go into a static lunge position: by bending the back knee, go down toward the floor until the front knee is bent at 90 degrees; the front knee should be in line with the foot and hip.
- Pelvis should remain level and the front knee should not come in front of the ankle.

Static lunge. COACH HOUSE PHYSIOTHERAPY CLINIC

- Return to the start by pushing the front heel down into the floor.
- Breathe in on the way down.

9B STATIC LUNGES TAKING ARMS OVER HEAD

- Go into a static lunge as above.
- Breathe in on the way down, at the same time as taking your arms over your head.
- Breathe out on the way back up, bringing the arms back by your sides; activate front gluts by pushing the front heel down into the floor, as you return to the start.
- Repeat 3 × 10 reps.

9C LUNGE ROTATIONS

- Go into a static lunge position as above.
- Keep the pelvis level.
- Place hands across chest. Breathe in on the way down into the lunge. Keeping spine tall and over pelvis, rotate upper

Static lunge. COACH HOUSE PHYSIOTHERAPY CLINIC

Lunge, arms over the head. COACH HOUSE PHYSIOTHERAPY CLINIC

back towards the side of the front knee.
- Rotate forward again so that you are facing forwards.
- Breathe out on the way back up to the start position; activate front gluts by pushing the front heel down into the floor, as you return to the start.
- Repeat 3 × 10 reps.

10. Dynamic Hops
- These are good for retraining dynamic contraction and elastic recoil of your calf

Lunge rotation. COACH HOUSE PHYSIOTHERAPY CLINIC

Dynamic hops. COACH HOUSE PHYSIOTHERAPY CLINIC

muscle, also for noticing differences in hop quality between left and right.

- Do two double foot bounces, and then one single hop on to your right foot, then double bounce again and repeat (that is, bounce, bounce, hop, bounce, bounce, hop).
- Can be done in different directions and at different jump heights to progress, as well as mixing left and right.
- This also makes a good warm-up exercise.
- Especially if coming back after injury, do small sets of 20–30sec, building up as able.

11. Hip Flexion

- Sit on a Swiss ball facing a mirror, with your sitting bones in centre of the ball and good posture.

Hip flexion. COACH HOUSE PHYSIOTHERAPY CLINIC

- Raise your right arm into the air and float right knee up, lifting your right foot off the floor.
- In doing this, your trunk should not deviate during the lift and your pelvis should stay level (wear kit so that you can check this).
- If this is difficult, start by just rolling your heel off the floor, or by lodging the ball in a corner against the wall, or do the exercise sitting on a chair.
- NB If this exercise is particularly difficult and there is a big difference left to right that does not improve, it would be advisable to see a physiotherapist for further advice.
- 3 sets of 5–10 reps on each side.

12. Abdominals

- Lie on your back with a small bend at the hips and knees (this helps ensure that the abdominals and not the hip flexor muscles are doing the work), with hands resting on the front of the thighs.
- Slide your hands towards the knees, with the trunk leaving the floor.
- When your fingertips reach the knees, the trunk should be slowly lowered back on to the floor, the hands moving back towards the hips.
- It is important to do these slowly and in a controlled fashion in order to get the strengthening benefits.
- It may be necessary to start with as few as 5 reps, building up to 20, doing 3 sets.
- This can be repeated with the thighs and legs bent to one side, this time the hands moving ahead into the space above the thighs to work the lateral abdominal muscles. Then move the thighs and legs to the opposite side of the body to work the opposite side. Again, start with 5 reps and 3 sets, increasing gradually to 20 reps as the muscles get stronger.

Abdominals. COACH HOUSE PHYSIOTHERAPY CLINIC

13. Endurance Combination Abdominals

- Lie on your back with your left leg straight on the floor and your right knee bent with foot on floor. Put your right hand behind your right ear.
- Contract your abdominals and lift your straight left leg just off the floor – feel the abdominals contract inside the left hip bone.
- Rotate the right elbow towards the left hip.
- Hold for 5sec and repeat 20 times on each side.
- Exhale each time you lift the elbow, inhaling on the return towards the floor.

Endurance combination abdominals. COACH HOUSE PHYSIOTHERAPY CLINIC

14. Raised Pec Stretch

- Stand facing the wall, with your arm out to the side with the elbow at 90 degrees and at shoulder height.
- Turn your chest and ribcage away from the wall/arm, keeping the front of your shoulder close to the wall. You should feel the stretch in the front of the shoulder.
- Repeat as above with your elbow at shoulder height and then with the elbow just above shoulder height.
- Hold both stretches for 30sec × 2.

Raised pec stretch. COACH HOUSE PHYSIOTHERAPY CLINIC

Raised pec stretch. COACH HOUSE PHYSIOTHERAPY CLINIC

Running Drills

Running drills can help you improve your running technique and hence running economy, as well as potentially reduce injury potential. Drills break your running action down into its component parts and are designed to make you more effective at recruiting nerves and muscles efficiently, something that can be particularly useful as you get older or when coming back from injury. They can be carried out either as part of an active warm-up or part of a session itself.

The downside of drills is that they are very easy to do incorrectly, which has the opposite effect to that desired, ingraining poor movement habits. For this reason, while promoting the value of drills, we do not include any individual drills in detail. Rather, we would recommend that if you are interested in incorporating running drills into your training, you seek advice and feedback from an appropriate coach, physiotherapist or physical trainer.

To get the most benefit from drills, remember:

1. Always be aware of your posture – this must be as perfect as possible for you.
2. Drills should be completed slowly to begin with. Speed should be added in only once the drill has been mastered.
3. It is important the drills are done well, as you are training a new skill. Even as you progress through the drills, always include some slow drills to ensure there are no bad habits creeping in.
4. Be specific and focused.

Balance

Balance is particularly important for trail, mountain and fell running and indeed for any running over uneven ground. While balance will improve naturally if you run over rough ground, there are additional exercises that can be done to help. This is particularly important for runners returning from injury, or who have an identified weakness. In these circumstances, going straight back to running on uneven ground carries the risk of placing too great a stress on the ankle, resulting in a reccurrence or new ankle injury.

Balance Training

Balance on one leg (alternating) and gradually increase the time you are able to stand before you lose your balance or your foot/ankle tires. When competent (and safe) doing this (about 5min per leg), progress to bouncing a ball against a wall while on one leg. This means that your mind is partly distracted and thus closer to the reality of running over rough ground (concentrating on running, where to put next foot plant, keeping an eye on the navigation, avoiding other runners), particularly when descending quickly.

There are various 'balance' boards and cushions available for doing this but these tend to be more useful when returning from injury rather than a necessity for preventative exercises. Once you are comfortable with the above, you can then move on to more dynamic exercises such as hopping- and bounding-based ones.

Stretching

Stretching is an area surrounded by controversy. Despite what is written in many running magazines, preached by fitness experts and practised by thousands of runners, there is no strong evidence to suggest stretching improves performance. Likewise, while it is considered valuable in reducing the risk of injury, and there is a theoretical basis to support such, there is no scientific research that confirms it does. Stretching may also be considered useful to help reduce post-activity muscle soreness as well as a tool to help lengthen muscle fibres.

The rationale behind stretching, as part of warm-up, is that it prepares the muscles for the stresses that are about to be placed upon them by running, be it in training or competition. Muscles go through episodic shortening and lengthening in order to bring about movement (as mentioned in Chapter 2). By stretching in advance, it theoretically prepares them for the activities ahead, something potentially more important in sprint events, but even in trail, mountain and fell running there may be a sprint start; for example, where there is a gate/bridge early on the course, which will produce a bottleneck, with valuable time being lost for those not at the front. Warming up, including stretching as preparation for racing, is covered in detail in Chapter 7. Dynamic stretches and dynamic movements, which make an ideal part of preparation before activity, should be done after a warm-up. They ideally should be done actively, while walking or jogging. This is because muscles are often likened to plasticine in that when they are warmer they are more malleable and less likely to break or tear.

For trail, mountain and fell runners, in addition to stretching the obvious leg muscle groups – calves, quadriceps, hamstrings – 'accessory' muscles should also be considered, in particular the thigh abductors and adductors, which may not be considered vital but are brought to attention when they cramp up in the later stages of an ultra.

Current consensus is that stretching as a tool to maintain or increase muscle length is best kept to after an activity, or carried out in specific stretching sessions, when the focus can be on holding slightly longer controlled stretches (never stretch beyond the point of discomfort). It is, however, a fallacy that runners should always do lots of stretching to become more flexible. Stretching should be done to ensure muscles are an optimum length for running at a below maximal pace. There is plenty of evidence to show that endurance runners tend not to be very flexible, and that being too flexible is potentially disadvantageous in terms of performance and injury. Stretching should therefore be done to help maintain muscle length, or increase it where muscle length is an identified performance limitation or injury risk.

It is possible to make use of foam rollers, tennis balls and other aids within a stretching routine, helping to ensure pressure is correctly applied to a particular soft-tissue area. Runners wishing to use such, should seek the advice of a physiotherapist or exercise specialist to ensure optimum use.

CHAPTER 4

ENJOYING THE ENVIRONMENT AND STAYING SAFE

Much of the attraction of trail, mountain and fell running is the environment within which it takes place. While for some it is about tackling terrain that is trickier and more demanding than running on 'boring' tarmac, for most trail, mountain and fell runners there is at least an element of enjoyment of the natural terrain within which they run. Space, freedom, tranquillity, peace, openness, beauty, magnificence are words often used by runners to describe their feelings and emotions about the environment they perform in. Others might describe it as raw, natural, harsh, wild, unspoilt, hostile, a challenge.

Whichever you side with, it is very hard to

Trail running in the Lake District. DAN VERNON/NOVA INTERNATIONAL

put into words quite what it is about trail and mountain running that means once it has hold of you it is hard to let go. Perhaps the most eloquent explanation for our love of the hills and things not man-made is in the book *Mountains of the Mind* by Robert Macfarlane, in which he attempts to describe much more vividly and in-depth than we do, man's fascination with the high mountains. We may not run in quite such vaulted places, but the ethos remains the same, and is also something fully captured in *Run Wild* by Boff Whalley, who is a great advocate for non-tarmac running.

If we are to continue to be able to enjoy this environment, whether it is for the challenge, the peacefulness, or both, then we need to know how to do so safely, be able to look after ourselves and in a way that leaves minimal traces of our presence.

Respecting the Environment

'Take only photos, leave only footprints' is a phrase reminding us to respect the environment in which we run. While recent legislative changes have given greater access to the open countryside, abusive, destructive or antisocial behaviour not only defaces the natural beauty we all want, but also puts future access and events at risk.

As a start, The Countryside Code should always be observed when out running or racing. It is perhaps easier to do this when running; when you are in 'the heat of battle', it can prove more difficult. There are, however, a number of races that have been threatened with discontinuation thanks to runners dropping litter (how much does carrying an empty gel wrapper really slow you down?), leaving gates open 'for the person behind to close' or being verbally abusive to other land users when asking them to move to one side.

The Countryside Code
(Reproduced from Natural England webpage with permission)

The Countryside Code applies to all parts of the countryside. Most of it is just good common sense, designed to help us all to respect, protect and enjoy our countryside. The Code, which applies in England and Wales, makes it clear what the responsibilities are for both the public and the people who manage the land. The Countryside Code started life in the 1950s as the Country Code. This version was launched in July 2004.

Code for the public
Five sections of The Countryside Code are dedicated to helping members of the public respect, protect and enjoy the countryside and these are given below:

1. Be safe, plan ahead and follow any signs
Even when going out locally, it's best to get the latest information about where and when you can go. For example, your rights to go on to some areas of open land may be restricted while work is carried out, for safety reasons, or during breeding seasons. Follow advice and local signs, and be prepared for the unexpected.

Continued overleaf

- Refer to up-to-date maps or guidebooks, for details of open access land visit the Natural England website or contact local information centres.
- You are responsible for your own safety and for others in your care, so be prepared for changes in weather and other events.
- Check weather conditions before you leave, and don't be afraid to turn back.
- Part of the appeal of the countryside is that you can get away from it all. You may not see anyone for hours, and there are many places without clear mobile phone signals, so let someone know where you're going and when you expect to return.
- Get to know the signs and symbols used in the countryside.

2. Leave gates and property as you find them

Please respect the working life of the country-side, as our actions can affect people's livelihoods, our heritage, and the safety and welfare of animals and ourselves.

- A farmer will normally leave a gate closed to keep livestock in, but may sometimes leave it open so they can reach food and water. Leave gates as you find them or follow instructions on signs. If walking in a group, make sure the last person knows how to leave the gates.
- If you think a sign is illegal or misleading such as a 'Private – No Entry' sign on a public footpath, contact the local authority.
- In fields where crops are growing, follow the paths wherever possible.
- Use gates, stiles or gaps in field boundaries when provided – climbing over walls, hedges and fences can damage them and increase the risk of farm animals escaping.
- Our heritage belongs to all of us – be careful not to disturb ruins and historic sites.
- Leave machinery and livestock alone – don't interfere with animals even if you think they're in distress. Try to alert the farmer instead.

3. Protect plants and animals and take your litter home

We have a responsibility to protect our coun-tryside now and for future generations, so make sure you don't harm animals, birds, plants or trees.

- Litter and leftover food doesn't just spoil the beauty of the countryside, it can be dangerous to wildlife and farm animals and can spread disease – so take your litter home with you. Dropping litter and dumping rubbish are criminal offences.
- Discover the beauty of the natural environ-ment and take special care not to damage, destroy or remove features such as rocks, plants and trees. They provide homes and food for wildlife, and add to everybody's enjoyment of the countryside.
- Wild animals and farm animals can behave unpredictably if you get too close, especially if they're with their young – so give them plenty of space.
- Fires can be as devastating to wildlife and habitats as they are to people and property – so be careful not to drop a match or smouldering cigarette at any time of the year. Sometimes, controlled fires are used to manage vegetation, particularly on heaths and moors between October and early April, so please check that a fire is not supervised before calling 999.

4. Keep dogs under close control

The countryside is a great place to exercise dogs, but it's every owner's duty to make sure their dog is not a danger or nuisance to farm animals, wildlife or other people.

- By law, you must control your dog so that it does not disturb or scare farm animals or wildlife. On most areas of open country and common land, known as 'access land', you must keep your dog on a short lead between 1 March and 31 July, and all year round near farm animals.

- You do not have to put your dog on a lead on public paths, as long as it is under close control. But as a general rule, keep your dog on a lead if you cannot rely on its obedience. By law, farmers are entitled to destroy a dog that injures or worries their animals.
- If a farm animal chases you and your dog, it is safer to let your dog off the lead – don't risk getting hurt by trying to protect it.
- Take particular care that your dog doesn't scare sheep and lambs or wander where it might disturb birds that nest on the ground and other wildlife – eggs and young will soon die without protection from their parents.
- Everyone knows how unpleasant dog mess is and it can cause infections – so always clean up after your dog and get rid of the mess responsibly. Also make sure your dog is wormed regularly to protect it, other animals and people.
- At certain times, dogs may not be allowed on some areas of access land or may need to be kept on a lead. Please follow any signs. You can also find out more by phoning the Open Access Contact Centre on 0845 100 3298.

5. Consider other people

Showing consideration and respect for other people makes the countryside a pleasant environment for everyone – at home, at work and at leisure.

- Busy traffic on small country roads can be unpleasant and dangerous to local people, visitors and wildlife – so slow down and, where possible, leave your vehicle at home, consider sharing lifts and use alternatives such as public transport or cycling.
- Respect the needs of local people – for example, don't block gateways, driveways or other entry points with your vehicle.
- Keep out of the way when farm animals are being gathered or moved and follow directions from the farmer.
- When riding a bike or driving a vehicle, slow down for horses, walkers and livestock and give them plenty of room. By law, cyclists must give way to walkers and horse-riders on bridleways.
- Support the rural economy – for example, buy your supplies from local shops.

The Responsible Trail, Mountain and Fell Runner's Race Rules

1. If a route goes through a gate or over a stile, use it; do not climb over the wall to one side. This might mean that you have to queue so, better still, use tactics to make sure that you reach the slowing point at the front of a group not the back.
2. Take your litter home with you: make every effort to put your empty gel wrappers and so on back into your bum bag, or stuff them down your vest or shorts.
3. When taking drinks from drinks stations, do not carry the cup for miles and then drop it; either drink quickly and drop it in the close vicinity of the drink station, or put it in your bum bag/rucksack and carry it to the finish.
4. Unless someone is directly behind you and they agree to shut it, shut gates as you go through them – if a runner is 100m behind you, there is plenty of time for sheep or other livestock to use the gate before they reach it.
5. Only take dogs on the race with the race organizer's permission.
6. Always carry the kit required by the

63

race organizer as a minimum; take more if you need to.

7. Where paths have been reinforced or man-made, stay on them; do not run to the side or cut the corners on zigzags.

8. If another runner is in trouble, stop and assist – make sure they are warm and either help them move or get help.

9. Be considerate with pre-race parking: use that provided by the organizer (even if you have to pay for it) rather than blocking or impeding local residents, and ideally travel two to four people to a car.

10. If the race has a set route, follow it, even if it is not marked; do not cut corners or take short cuts, especially across private farmland.

11. Think before you pee… use public or provided toilets and leave plenty of time to do so; the sight of half-dressed grown men and women dashing in and out of local bushes, particularly in residential areas, is likely to lead to complaints to the race organizers.

12. Respect other countryside users. Generally, walkers and others are very considerate in letting runners go past, but be courteous and maintain the 'good name' of trail, mountain and fell running.

Good-natured queuing at a stile during a race. DAVE WOODHEAD

Personal Safety

Much is written in running magazines about personal safety, especially for female runners, normally coming from the angle of being vulnerable to attack from another human. This unfortunately is often magnified when referring to running off-road and in woods or more isolated terrain, the result being that many runners feel worried, in our view unnecessarily, about the risks and dangers of running off-road.

This is not to suggest that you should be blasé about things; it is always wise to be cautious and be aware of your surroundings (see the section below on basic safety fundamentals). Having said that, in our combined circa seventy years of running experience on road, off-road, in cities, in villages, in parks and open spaces and in remote areas of wilderness, neither of us have ever been, or felt, personally threatened by another person when enjoying the trail- and mountain-running environment. Yes, we have and continue to experience the odd comment (some ruder or funnier than others) when running on local canal banks or through urban parks but, as a general rule, the people whom you meet when out on the trails and mountains are fellow lovers of the environment they are in, even if doing so at a slower pace than you!

Safety Fundamentals

If you want to run and enjoy the countryside, and to do so without putting yourself or others at undue risk, then it is about running within your limits of expertise. There are runners who have the skills and experience to be able to head off in midwinter, alone, and successfully complete 24-hour traverses of Scottish mountain ranges in severe weather conditions. These people are the exception and will normally have built up years of experience to be competent to do this.

Most runners will never aspire to quite that level of adventure. There is, however, no reason why all runners should not be able to head out for a run off the tarmac and away from civilization. It is a case of being sensible and making sure that the route you choose is appropriate for your skills and experience. With time, and as you gain more confidence and a better understanding of the demands and risks, so you will be able to explore further, wilder and higher, safely, should you want to.

It does not take much to be able to really enjoy trails and mountains, and it is hard to beat running through virgin snow on a crisp winter's day; at the same, it should not be forgotten that in poor weather there has been the occasional loss of life among runners.

Safety Guidelines

1. If heading out alone, tell someone where you are going and approximately for how long, or leave a note to the same effect.
2. Plan your route taking into account the weather, not just as it is, but also what is predicted – if you are planning going up into the hills, make sure that you have options to be able to cut back down to lower ground if you need to.
3. Have the basic navigational skills to know where you are (see next section); do not rely on either using your mobile phone or GPS watch as your safety method. Mobile-phone reception is frequently poor, or non-existent in remote or high places.
4. Make sure you have the knowledge and kit to be able keep warm should you trip or fall (see below) and, as a minimum, carry an extra windproof layer or top – it is amazing how quickly

the body chills when you suddenly stop running for any length of time. In all but the hottest of weathers on any long run, SR always carries a lightweight Pertex top with her; it weighs next to nothing and has come in very handy on occasions when the 50min run home has turned into a 2hr slow hobble due to an unfortunate ankle twist.

5. Likewise, if there is any danger that you are going to be out when the light starts to go, take a head torch. Unfortunately, many are the times when optimistic planning means great days out take slightly longer than planned. Should this happen, it is much easier if all the group have head torches, not just one or none of you.

6. Other basics to think about taking with you if planning a long trip out are phone, money and something to eat and drink. While old-fashioned, a whistle is still the best way to attract attention if you are injured or in trouble.

7. Be aware of your surroundings, many runners like to listen to music via headphones when they run. The downside of this is that you lose the ability to use one of our key warning senses, namely sound. Wearing headphones means you will not hear others approaching you from behind and has led to cases of people not hearing a train at an unmanned railway crossing as well as not hearing traffic noise when on bikes. More pertinent perhaps for trail, mountain and fell runners is the warning sign where a trail joins a private farm track in Leicestershire: 'Please remove ear phones when joining the lane and beware of cars and tractors', put up as a result of a number of unfortunate but fully avoidable accidents.

8. Leave animals alone, particularly young ones who may look like they are on their own. The likelihood is that there will be a very maternal parent not too far away, and 500kg of fast-moving angry cow. Do not get between a cow and her young as that can cause the mother to attack, especially if you have a dog with you. It is much better to give the herd a wide berth. Remember also that young animals or birds become tainted with human smell and may then be abandoned by their parents.

9. If it looks dangerous to you, then it is! Do not get pulled into a feeling of bravado, doing or going somewhere because someone else has done so. Take particular care if you are alone. If you do not like the look of a steep slope/deep river/snow slope, then do not cross it. It is important to use your senses: look out for visual hazards and listen for warning sounds.

10. Finally, do not rely on your mobile phone to get you out of trouble. While they can be useful to alert friends and family if you are running overdue and hence avoid an unnecessary call-out of mountain rescue services, they should not be viewed as a fail-safe safety measure. Reception is often a problem and battery life is adversely affected by the cold; therefore, other resources should be considered far more important and mobile phones merely an adjunct. Likewise, modern smartphones with built-in GPS should not replace taking a map and compass (with all members carrying these when in a group). In many people's minds, any subsequent call out of the mountain rescue service in such circumstances due to being lost, is an inappropriate use of this valuable and voluntary

service, which should be used only for genuine emergencies.

Those wanting to run in remote places should focus as much as possible on being self-sufficient. This means having kit appropriate to the terrain and weather, and the skills to be able to know where you are and to get back to civilization.

First Aid Fundamentals

In Chapter 6, we explore injury and injury prevention for trail, mountain and fell runners in more detail. By nature of the environment within which it takes place, those who run on trails, mountains and fells should also have a sound knowledge of basic first aid.

Immunization As prevention is better than cure, remember to ensure that your immunization against tetanus is up to date. Most people in the UK will be covered as a result of childhood immunization, but a 'dirty' cut, wound or animal bite might warrant a 'booster' dependent on when the initial immunization occurred.

Cuts should be cleaned and covered. On the hill it may be a question of using whatever is available or what you have with you, but back at base an antiseptic cleanser should be used and ideally a scrubbing brush to remove grit (the world is now such that in a Mountain Marathon, a few years ago, when first aiders were approached to assist with a dirty wound, a scrubbing brush was handed out to the runner to 'get on with it'!).

Bruises/strains/sprains Cold should be applied when possible. There may be a mountain stream to hand or it may have to wait until back at base. If using a cold pack, remember to avoid ice burns by wrapping it up in a wet towel.

Blisters Compeed or equivalent may be useful to cover and protect. An alternative,

especially if the blister is still only a 'hot spot', is to add a layer of zinc oxide tape over the offending area. Whether to pierce the blister or not will depend on the site and whether facilities are available to do it under clean conditions. In the middle of an event, it is probably sensible not to, as it will be painful initially and there is a risk of infection. However, if you have a day or two in hand, the quickest solution is to pierce to allow the two main layers of skin to adhere together as soon as possible.

Knowing Where You Are

A map and compass may be 'foreign' to the road runner trying trail, mountain and fell running for the first time, but they are essentials, particularly if you are in an unknown area

Using a map and compass during a race. DAVE WOODHEAD

where there may be no paths or a plethora of them – in the latter case, to ensure that you are on the correct one!

Before readers play down the need to be able to use a map and compass because they know where they are, it is well worth remembering that it is not uncommon for top British fell runners, racing over complex terrain they know and have raced over for years, such as in the Lake District, to go wrong – often much to the delight of their competitors. Particularly if the mist is down, it is exceptionally easy to veer slightly off the correct path and, before you know it, find yourself on the wrong peak or in the wrong valley. This can easily be avoided by having a compass and a known bearing.

If you are unlucky enough to get injured or if fatigued, it is easy to become disoriented and need the quickest/safest way down/back to base. If you want to take part in British fell races, then all races of medium or long duration require you to carry a map and compass and, ideally, know how to use them. Having the attitude of 'It's OK, I will follow someone else' is both foolish and potentially dangerous, not least in the case when the mist is down and you can see no more than 5 or 10 metres in front. Remember that getting the most enjoyment from the trails and mountains comes with a degree of personal responsibility.

For these reasons, it is very important to know how to use a map and compass, even if you like to use a GPS watch to guide your way, not least because some races ban the use of GPSs (see the section on GPS in Chapter 5). There are numerous ways to develop map and compass skills, practice and trial and error in local known areas being one, especially if the area has a fixed orienteering course. Other alternatives are linking with a local orienteering club or, for more specific mountain and fell proficiency, the Fell Runners

Association (FRA) run two navigational courses a year and the Outward Bound (OB) many more, as increasingly do commercial organizations. Some athletic clubs do navigation work in summer.

It is important to remember that there are numerous maps both in terms of make and scale, with different symbols and colours. Some well-established fell races and long trail races, such as the Ultra Tour of the Lake District, produce specific maps of the route, either for sale or as part of the entry fee (you, of course, still need to be able to use them!).

It is beyond the scope of this book to go into details as to how to use a map and compass, over and above the core basics – rather we would, in the strongest possible language, encourage all runners who want to be proficient trail, mountain and fell runners to ensure they know how to use a compass and to read a map.

While at first glance navigation might seem daunting, once you have the basics it is both great fun and at times frustrating: fun because it means you can add an extra dimension to your running knowing you have the skills to go further afield safely; frustrating because all great navigators without exception make mistakes at times, we do still and you will – the challenge when this happens is using your skills to relocate back to where you want to be!

Navigation Basics

- On maps, natural features are relatively stable, but manmade features can change and are occasionally marked incorrectly.
- Remember that rivers and streams always run downhill – obvious, but perhaps forgotten when wanting to get off a hill quickly in the cold and failing light.
- As well as noting the scale of the map (1:50,000 means that 1cm on the

map represents 500m on the ground; 1:25,000 means 1cm on the map represents 250m on the ground), it is important to note the contour interval. This is usually 10m or 15m, the important feature being that when contours are close together it is a steep slope; when they are more widely spaced, it is less steep.

- The two most widely used makes of maps are Ordnance Survey and Harveys. Although the universal symbols will be the same, others, plus colouring, may differ. Make sure you know how features are represented and that the straight-line path you want to follow on the map is not, in reality, a parish boundary line!
- Except in a few places in the Scottish Highlands, the moving red part of the needle of a compass will always point north.
- A grid reference is a six-figure number that enables you to locate a position on a map to within 100m (or an eight-figure grid reference, which will be more precise, but rarely necessary). A feature will have the same grid reference whatever the make or scale of map.
- Ideally, plan an 'escape route' in advance so that if you are in difficulty or running out of time or daylight you can get down safely.

For those who want to read further on navigational skills we would recommend the following:

Bagness, Martin, *Mountain Navigation for Runners*. Misty Fell Books (ISBN 0 95210 050 9). A very detailed guide.
McNeil, Carol, *Orienteering*. The Crowood Press (ISBN 978 1 84 797206 4). Covers all key aspects of the sport of orienteering, including navigation.
Mee, Pat and Brian, *Outdoor Navigation,*

Handbook for Tutors. Harveys (ISBN 978 1 85 137002 3). Concentrates on the practical aspects of teaching navigation and map reading outdoors.
Rowell, Sarah, *Off-Road Running*. The Crowood Press (ISBN 978 1 86126 523 4). This covers the basics of map and compass work.

Factoring in the Weather

All runners, wherever they run, should take account of the weather, what it is currently doing and what it is forecast to do. When running on trails and mountains, this becomes more important for two reasons. First, if something does go wrong or the weather turns much worse than you expected, you are likely to be further away from shelter or assistance compared with running in a built-up area. Second, the very nature of where you run means the weather conditions have the ability to be more severe.

Cold

When running on a cold and damp day, most runners are fine with a couple of layers on top, a pair of long or three-quarter leggings and maybe hat and gloves. This is because the body is a pretty inefficient machine, losing up to 70 per cent of the energy it generates as heat, meaning that while moving you stay warm with only a few layers on. The downside, of course, is that as soon as you stop, you chill and quickly get cold. For this reason, when running in the cold (or even semi-cold), or when going out for several hours, we would always recommend that you take as a minimum a spare upper body layer (normally a windproof). If, for some reason, you have to slow or stop – for example, due to injury or getting lost – you will rapidly cool down. Even during a race in standard summer UK conditions, if injured it is important to put on

Well dressed to enjoy the winter conditions. TRISS KENNY

additional clothing as soon as possible, as the body rapidly cools. Doing so is likely to take precedence over seeking injury treatment in all but the most serious of cases.

Runners should always be aware that benign, warm conditions in a valley or at sea level will not mean the same once you get higher up, where it will more than likely be windier and cooler – great in the heat of a hot summer but potentially dangerous on a dull spring or autumn day. Wind increases the loss of body heat with the 'wind chill' factor (the combined effect of low temperature and wind, for which predictive charts are available – see below) accounting for up to 80 per cent of heat loss in cold conditions. If, in addition to being windy it is also wet, then this adds

further to the cooling effect. In extreme cases, this can lead to hypothermia.

Hypothermia

Hypothermia is always a potential risk when in the mountains as weather conditions can change suddenly and, as well as being aware of your own possible symptoms (see the box below), you should also be alert to these occurring in running companions. If hypothermia is suspected, or even general chilling, more clothing should be put on after ideally removing any wet layers (here vanity should go out of the window in terms of being helped to get your wet gear off and dry clothes on). If shelter can be reached, then it should be used while the sufferer is warmed

Table 12: Wind–Chill–Factor Effect

Wind Speed (mph)	Temperature (degrees C)					
	20	12	4	−4	−12	−20
4	18	9	0	−6	−18	−28
12	16	5	−5	−16	−26	−37
20	15	3	−8	−19	−31	−42
28	14	2	−10	−21	−33	−47
36	13	1	−11	−23	−35	−47
42	13	1	−11	−23	−35	−48
48	13	1	−11	−24	−36	−48
54	13	1	−11	−24	−36	−48

gradually and, if she or he is conscious, given warm drinks. If you are on a mountain or high up, you should get down as quickly as possible while staying safe, as the temperature will be warmer lower down, and make your way to safety. The one situation when rapid warming is used is after sudden cold-water immersion, hopefully an unlikely scenario in trail, mountain and fell running.

Bad conditions can occur at any time of year in the hills and mountains. ANDY HOLDEN

Warning Signs for Hypothermia

Shivering

Tinges of blue around the extremities

Grey skin colour

Bizarre behaviour

Slurred speech

Memory difficulty

Unsteadiness

Drowsiness and/or fatigue

There may also be denial of symptoms as the effort involved in putting on more clothes may be more than the victim can cope with.

Heat

That the body loses most of the energy it generates as heat might help us stay warm in the cold, but this is not so helpful when exercising in the heat. Our bodies are, however, well designed to dissipate heat (there is one chain of thought that this dates back to our ancestry and the need to hunt animals by long chases in hot or warm weather in Africa). We do this in a number of ways: convection, conduction, radiation and evaporation. While at rest, the first three contribute to around 80 per cent of heat lost from the body; during exercise, evaporation (through sweating) becomes much more important, accounting for up to 80 per cent of the heat lost. This is even more important when the air temperature rises to about 37°C and hence warmer than body temperature. At these temperatures, the body absorbs (rather than loses) heat from the atmosphere through convection, conduction and radiation.

It is not the process of sweating that helps to keep us cool; rather, it is when sweat evaporates off our skin. In order to help regulate against overheating due to a combination of the heat we produce while exercising combined with the environmental heat around us, our bodies produce sweat, which, as it evaporates from the skin, helps cool the body. If the sweat only drips off, then there is limited subsequent heat loss. This is what happens when the humidity increases – the amount of water in the air means it is more difficult for sweat to evaporate rather than drip off. In these conditions, heat loss by convection and radiation becomes relatively more important.

The greater the intensity of exercise, the more heat the body produces and, in turn, the more we have to sweat to get rid of the heat. At the same time, the blood vessels in the skin dilate, bringing an increased blood flow to the skin. As much as 2 litres of sweat can be produced in an hour, which has significant implications for fluid replacement.

If air temperature is over 37°C and relative humidity is 70 per cent or above, then the conditions mean that the body stores the heat generated by exercise. This can occur in many European countries in the summer months and is more likely the further south you travel. Heat issues may also be a challenge in Africa, Asia, North America, South America and Australasia, depending on the time of year. Thus, if you are planning to race in other countries, it is worth checking on the likely climatic conditions for the race. Remember, however, that in mountainous areas not only can weather be unpredictable, but the higher the altitude, the cooler the temperature. In the 2006 Ultra-Trail Tour du Mont-Blanc (held at the end of August), it was warm enough to wear only shorts and a vest for most of the first twenty-four hours, with heat being an issue during the middle of the day despite going above 2,500m; yet in 2010, the race was cancelled because of the rain and snow.

When running in the heat, clothing should be light, both in weight and colour, loose fitting and with a loose weave to help sweat evaporation. Alternatively, some runners will prefer to use tighter fitting hi-tech fabrics, which are designed to transfer the sweat away from your body.

The UK may seem a long way from Africa, but during hot weather all runners should take simple precautions to ensure they do not suffer from heat stress or worse:

- Make sure that you have access to enough fluid – normally by carrying it, or knowing where you can get hold of supplies via shops, taps or fresh running water from streams (for more on how much to drink see Chapter 6).
- Ensure you have ways of protecting your

skin from the sun by wearing light-coloured clothing (white reflects heat; black absorbs heat), designed to wick sweat away from the body, as well as a sun hat with visor and potentially a mesh neck cover.

- Sunglasses with UV protection should be used to reduce the glare, particularly at altitude, and if crossing snow, where reflection of the sun will be more prominent (it is possible to get sunburn of the conjunctiva – the outer covering of the eye – and, even worse, snow blindness).
- Sunscreen designed for physical activity with a high sun-protection factor (SPF) should be used.
- Avoid running in the heat of midday, and/or use routes which have plenty of shade.

For those who have races planned in hot environments, then time spent acclimatizing to the heat beforehand will make a big difference on race day. If lucky, this can be done by travelling to the race venue seven to ten days beforehand and then training at least every other day during the hotter part of the day. If you are not able to do this, then 'DIY' can be done at home by running in additional kit at the hottest part of the day or making use of saunas/heat chambers, if available (Don Thompson, the British walker who won an Olympic gold medal in 1960 at the Rome Olympic Games, trained for it by walking on the spot in his bathroom with a heater and wearing a full tracksuit). As you acclimatize to the heat, you will find that you start to sweat sooner, that you sweat more and it is more dilute – all positive signs of adaptation.

Dressed to tackle the heat and sand of the Marathon des Sables. HILARY BLOOR

Signs of Heat Stress

Headache
Fatigue
Dizziness
Tingling skin
Weak, rapid pulse
Nausea or vomiting
Pale and moist cool skin
Shivering

Hyperthermia

Should heat stress or hyperthermia occur, the key things to do are:

- Rehydrate, ideally using a solution with some sugar and electrolyte in it (an energy drink), though water will do. In rare cases, if the victim is unable to drink, intravenous fluid replacement may be required.
- Cool the sufferer with ice packs or wet towels, in a shaded area and, if available, using fans to increase convection.

When You Need to Go

This is perhaps a delicate subject, but one which is probably unavoidable, certainly if you want to run for any length of time on trails where there are no public toilets. What do you do? If you just need to pass urine, whether you are male or female the trick is doing so in a manner so as not to offend others, in other words, out of view. You should also ensure that in choosing your spot, it is not one where your urine will run directly into free-flowing water. Most women will wish to squat to pee, although doing so standing up is just as easy, if unconventional. If squatting, it is best to make sure you do so in an area void of stinging nettles or other such plants. The other advantage of standing is a reduction in the time and accessibility of bare flesh to midges and other biting insects in the evening.

When and if the urge to defecate arises, trail, mountain and fell runners should, if at all possible, pay a bit more time and attention. There are some areas where 'bagging' and bringing out is requested. Normally it is enough to make sure you are well away from sources of habitation and drinking water and that you can bury your waste and any toilet paper a good 10cm underground, ideally burning any toilet paper.

CHAPTER 5

KIT, SHOES AND EQUIPMENT

Compared with many sports, running may be considered 'cheap' to do, with the basic requirements being running shoes and appropriate clothing. To gain the most from your running, and especially trail, mountain and fell running, there are a few more essentials that will make it both more enjoyable and safer. Added to these, there are the various 'nice to haves' – GPS (Global Positioning System), altimeter, poles – to be considered. All of these will be covered in this chapter.

When considering any item, it is always important to think carefully about what use you want from it, whether shoes, rucksack or compass. There is plenty of variety on the market, with different products designed to suit different requirements. It is always worth making sure that you take the time first to work out what it is you want the piece of kit to do, or how you plan to use it and, second, do some research to marry that with the right product – which may mean borrowing from a friend to try before you buy. For example, even something as simple as a waterproof jacket gives plenty of options. Making sure you think about what features you want, followed up by some homework on the different products on the market will help ensure you get the right kit and equipment for what you need.

Footwear

Runners have always run 'off-road', if not racing then certainly in training, and were doing so long before shoes were specifically designed and marketed for this purpose. Indeed, if you look at the feet of runners in many trail and mountain races you will see plenty who are tackling the event in 'ordinary road shoes'. What need, then, for a whole genre of specialist shoes?

Perhaps the first running shoes designed for off-road events (other than cross-country spikes) were made by Norman Walsh, for the then niche market of British guide and fell racers in the north of the country in the1960s. By the late 1990s, most of the major running-shoe manufacturers were experimenting with off-road running shoes, as were a number of the outdoor- and climbing-focused companies.

While some of the early versions produced were not very suitable for purpose, at the time of writing trail, mountain and fell runners are spoilt for choice. There are currently over thirty different companies producing shoes designed to run in off-road. So how to choose ones that are best for you? As with any piece of kit, there are two things to consider: what do you want the shoes to do and what are your individual needs? This latter point has always been important when buying running shoes, given the individual differences in running style and therefore demands made on the foot. It is especially pertinent at present given the current push by shoe companies and various 'gurus' for minimalist or barefoot running.

The theory behind minimalist running may on one level make absolute sense: namely, going back to our early ancestry, enabling the bones and soft tissues of the feet and lower legs to function as they were supposedly designed for, hence giving you a better feel for the ground and enabling a more natural foot strike to occur. For some runners, adopting such an approach may suit them very well. For many others, though, the assistance and support provided by a more traditional running shoe will make the difference between running and being injured. This is not to say that support is always good; modern running shoes have, however, moved away from the heavy, bulked-up anti-pronation shoes of not so long ago, which is positive.

It is beyond the realms of this book to look in detail at the biomechanics of the running cycle. In short, the natural running gait involves an airborne phase and a support phase. The support element has three phases: foot strike, mid-support and take-off, with the foot going through a pattern of supination, neutral foot stance and pronation as you land, stabilize and then push off for the next stride, respectively. At the same time, there is shock absorption through the fore and rear foot.

In practice, very few runners have a perfect theoretical foot plant (including elite ones) and, for this reason, all the major shoe companies make road and now off-road shoes with different levels of motion control. If you are unsure about your running gait and which style of shoe would best suit you, we would recommend that you visit a specialist running-shoe retailer and get them to assess your running style.

What are the other things to consider when choosing a shoe for running on trails, mountains and fells? Starting with the very basic question of whether you need a different shoe from that worn for running on the roads, very often the answer will be no. If the trails are dry, not that rocky or not requiring much lateral foot movement and you have strong ankles, there are plenty of running shoes sold as road shoes that will do the job.

As the events get rougher, wetter, boggier and steeper, then there are good reasons to go for a specialist shoe. In addition to the things you would consider for a road-based shoe, namely cushioning, ride, flexibility, support and weight, when thinking about trail, mountain and fell running you also need to think about several other factors.

Tread

The nature of the running you do will alter the tread you want: wet, boggy land or steep grass require a more aggressive tread, with deeper lugs spaced apart to stop the mud congealing underneath, as typically found on fell-running shoes. Trail shoes tend to have a deeper tread than those designed for road running, but not as deep a tread as shoes designed for fell running.

Grip

How well do the shoes hold or stick to rock, especially wet rock or paving slabs? This will depend on the rubber compound used for

Motion Control

Motion control is the term for the amount of support the shoe gives to help control the foot from when it lands on the ground through to toe-off. While the neutral foot strike during running is to land in a slightly supinated position, rolling into mid-foot plant and then on to a slightly pronated position at toe-off, runners with poor motion control typically overpronate or sometimes over-supinate. Shoes designed to provide motion control have additional support to prevent this excessive movement, either on the inside of the shoe to control or limit pronation, or on the outside for excessive supination.

the sole; typically, the harder the rubber used, the more durable the sole (in that the studs will wear down less) but the less grip the shoe will have on rock. Alternatively, with softer rubber, the shoe will grip better especially on wet rock, but will also wear out quicker.

If running in snow or ice, then orienteering-style shoes, which may have small metal spikes built into the ends of the rubber lugs, can be helpful. There are a number of shoe manufacturers now making shoes specifically designed for running in snow and ice.

Alternatively, lightweight microspikes can quickly and easily transform an ordinary running shoe into one able to cope with such conditions. Consisting of steel spikes/chain with a tough elastic harness that fits over the shoe, they are lightweight and can easily be carried in a bum bag or rucksack and then quickly slipped over your shoes when required.

Profile

The profile of a shoe refers to how close to the ground your foot sits. Low-profile shoes provide a much flatter foot position due to a thinner mid-sole, where the difference in thickness between heel and toe is less. For off-road running, a lower-profile shoe tends to be preferable, giving a more stable foot plant when running on what is often an unstable and constantly changing surface. Lower-profile running shoes not only help you 'feel' the ground better, they can also help reduce the likelihood of acute injury caused by twisting or going over on your ankle. The downside of this is that lower-profile shoes tend to be less well cushioned and can put a greater strain on your Achilles tendon/calf muscle.

Protection

Does the shoe provide you with additional protection to protect your feet from loose rocks as well as from stubbing your toes on

fixed ones? Some off-road shoes have a built-up toe box and thicker rand (the strip of rubber that joins the sole to the outer) to help prevent stone bruising as well as to help stop sand and grit getting into the shoe and causing blisters. This additional protection tends to come at the expense of extra weight and often a less flexible shoe.

For races over (or through) sand and fine gravel, a shoe with a non-mesh upper is needed to prevent the fine grains getting into your shoe where they are likely to cause blisters. In addition, a small gaiter can and should be used.

Fit

If you are running on serious off-road surfaces with lots of ascents, descents and lateral foot movement, your foot will tend to move around in the shoe more, giving greater risk of blisters and bruised or sore toes. Shoes designed for fell running have a much tighter, narrower fit, giving a snug feeling, to prevent this, as do some trail-based ones.

Waterproofing

It is possible to buy waterproof running shoes. These may be useful for keeping your feet dry through wet grass or from the occasional puddle, but are of little use in really bad conditions, when the water will get in through the top and lace holes. If the water does get in, then it cannot easily drain out from the shoe due to the waterproofing of the upper. At best, this will mean your feet are being kept slightly warm by a layer of warm water; at worst, they will become soft, soggy and susceptible to blisters and tears. Waterproof shoes also tend to be heavier and less flexible owing to the fabric used for the upper.

Ankle Support

There are a number of running shoes on the market that resemble more of a lightweight

Mountainous terrain such as the Lake District requires specialist footwear. ANDY HOLDEN

boot, with built-up ankle support. Potential advantages of these are support for the ankle as well as added protection. The downside is that they tend to be restrictive to the natural running action of the foot.

Runners who wear orthortics may struggle to fit them into some of the pure fell shoes due to the narrower last and, in some cases, the shoe having a non-detachable inner.

While there is much crossover in shoes, in simple terms, on a continuum:

- Road shoes have a wider fit, the heel is more built up, there is greater cushioning and options to have motion control as required.
- Trail shoes have a wider fit, a semi-aggressive tread, protective toe cap and rand, good cushioning, a medium profile and some motion control.
- Fell shoes have a snug fit, low profile, aggressive tread, protective toecap and rand, limited cushioning and motion control.

Clothing

Sports clothing is an area of continuous design and innovation. Most is now made from technical manmade fabrics designed to wick sweat away from the body, while more recent advances include compression panels to support specific muscles, a move back to wool-based products, clothing with built-in odour protection or with a layer of reflective material to help with heat retention in the cold or provide UV protection. When considering clothing for trail, mountain and fell running, the principles that apply to normal running kit apply: comfort, fit, safety and functionality. There are a few additional things to think about to make sure that comfort and functionality, in particular, apply and this section should be read in conjunction with the section on Factoring in the Weather in Chapter 4.

Regarding functionality, layering is important; it is much better to wear or have available two to three layers of clothing, especially for the top half of your body, as opposed to one heavier layer. This ensures that you have more flexibility regarding temperature control, depending on how fast you are moving, how high or exposed you are and what the weather is doing. Layers of clothing trap air in-between them. As air is a poor conductor of heat, this aids insulation against the cold. Unless the weather is particularly bad, three layers – base layer, mid-layer and wind or waterproof layer – should normally suffice.

Underwear

What you wear next to skin is very much a personal preference, with the advice below about base layers also applicable. Perhaps the most important consideration is the location of seams, especially if you plan to be using a rucksack. If care is not taken, friction burns from the adjustments on the straps can occur. Some runners will put tape over potential pressure or sensitive areas. This is perhaps more important for women, although men can be seen taping nipples to avoid friction from clothing. For females, a variety of sports bras are available and should always be worn in preference to an ordinary bra for running, both to reduce excessive breast movement as well as increase comfort. Studies show that there is up to 12cm of breast movement if

running bare-chested with a D cup size. Sports bras without any fasteners are preferable for use if you are planning on running with a rucksack.

Base Layers

Here wicking qualities are key. Wicking is the process by which sweat is drawn away from the skin, helping to keep it dry. This helps with cooling in warmer conditions, as well as maintaining body warmth in cooler ones, by reducing the chilling effect of wet material. In winter, warmth/insulation also needs to be taken into consideration. Cotton is best avoided as it holds sweat. Synthetic materials transport sweat away quickly and spread it over the surface to speed up evaporation. There are plenty of different options: synthetic or increasingly wool; it is a case of personal preference.

As with underwear, seams are an important consideration regarding chafing, the more so the longer the event or the hotter the conditions. The closer the fit, the better the base layer is for wicking away sweat, but looser garments may be more comfortable and allow air to circulate in warmer conditions.

Finally, it is a case of deciding on the thickness and hence warmth/weather proofing, according to the event. The ideal is to have several options in order to be able to choose according to weather conditions on the day.

The choice of bottoms is a little less controversial. Traditional shorts remain popular, though tighter-fitting Lycra is ever more evident and gives more options with regards length, weather conditions, time of year and whether the event continues after dark. If conditions are very cold and wet, long leggings should be considered. It is also easier to run in long bottoms than in waterproof ones. Three-quarter-length leggings are often used by runners as a compromise and in some races are allowed to count as manda-

Altering clothing layers en route. ANDY HOLDEN

tory long leggings in terms of required kit. Leggings should always be made of Lycra or equivalent and reasonably tight-fitting, especially if rain is expected. Trackster-style bottoms may look more aesthetic on certain figures, but trying to run while holding up a pair of water-sodden trousers is neither fun nor effective.

Mid-Layers

A mid-layer is just that, a layer of clothing that you add over your base layer. Typically, a mid-layer is heavier and warmer than a base layer, often being of wool or brushed fleece. In warmer conditions, a long-sleeved T-shirt can double up as one or the other (base or mid-layer). If the core purpose of the base layer is comfort and helping keep the skin dry, then the mid-layer provides additional insulation.

Waterproofs

A waterproof top is probably the most important investment that, after shoes, a trail, mountain and fell runner will make, particularly in a British climate. Although many products claim to be waterproof, it is always difficult to find a garment that does fully protect, particularly at the lightweight end of the spectrum. For breathable waterproofs, Gore-tex remains the benchmark against which to judge others, with eVent another popular choice. It is possible to get a Gore-tex or other waterproof top weighing under 150g; however, they come at a cost and tend to be less durable. In choosing which jacket to buy, given the cost and range available, it is certainly worth doing some research, in particular considering:

- *Weight* – the lighter the jacket, even if made from Gore-Tex or equivalent, the less durable it is.
- *Length* – do you want the jacket to fully cover your backside or be waist length?
- *Sleeves* – are they long enough and do you want thumb loops to help keep your hands dry/warm?
- *Hood* – do you want a hood, either attached or detachable?
- *Pockets* – do you want side or chest pockets? Can you access your pockets if carrying a rucksack?
- *Zip* – do you want a full-length zip or half-length? The former tend to be heavier but provide more temperature control options, the latter lighter.
- *Fit* – how well fitting do you want the jacket to be? Think about how many layers you will want to wear underneath and make sure it is comfortable when running and moving in the hills; women should look for a women's specific fit.
- *Packability* – how easily does the jacket fit into a bum bag for carrying while running?
- *Waterproofing* – if the jacket is fully waterproof, taped seams are essential.

Breathable waterproof bottoms are less critical; however, if conditions are very bad and you are planning on being out for more than a few hours, lightweight waterproof bottoms should be carried.

Many British fell and longer mountain races require competitors to carry full body waterproofs with taped seams. Here runners tend to go for a reasonably high-spec waterproof and breathable jacket, but often bottoms that are waterproof but less breathable and hence cheaper.

Dressed for the conditions: Marco de Casperi at the Elbrus SkyRace. VICTORIA KLIMENKO

Adverse weather conditions and remaining safe are covered in Chapter 4, but it is worth remembering that runners have and continue to have to drop out of races or be rescued from the hills in bad conditions due to hypothermia, which could have been avoided by the use of adequate kit.

Windproofs

Unless you are on high exposed ground for much of the time, in Britain and certainly Europe a full waterproof is too hot to run in for any length of time, even if it is raining hard. A lightweight Pertex or equivalent top or gilet is excellent for adding a windproof layer in these conditions, or for just carrying 'in case' while running on the hills and trails. Pertex bottoms, while infrequently used, are also a handy reserve to have in your rucksack or bum bag when out on the hills in case of emergencies.

Socks

Socks are very much a personal preference and usually mixed fibre or pure wool are favoured, depending on the conditions. In colder, wetter conditions waterproof socks are useful in helping keep feet warm. It is unlikely, however, they will keep the feet dry in anything wetter than damp conditions; rather, they have the same effect as a wetsuit, helping trap a layer of warmer water. The downside is that your feet are, in effect, encased in water for some time, which can lead to softening and blisters/small tears if not careful.

Hats

Hats are valuable for reducing heat loss. A lightweight fleece variety is usually adequate or a 'buff' can be used and is more versatile, as is a balaclava. Waterproof hats are useful in really bad weather, and having a chinstrap or other holding device is also advised to make sure it stays on when very windy.

A hat or head cover is also sensible in sunny weather, especially for those who are fair skinned, have less hair, or who know they 'suffer' in the heat. A light-coloured baseball-style cap is best, ideally made from material that is heat reflective and has added UVF protection. In extreme heat, a mesh back to keep the sun off your neck is worth considering.

Gloves

Gloves of varying thickness and material can be invaluable when it is cold and wet. When your hands are cold and fingers numb, it is difficult to do even simple things like open and close gates, take or add things to a rucksack, let alone to manipulate a compass if navigation is required. If conditions are bad or have the potential to be so, gloves should always be taken. Windproof material is useful in helping to keep fingers warm if not dry, while reasonably tough fabric is useful if you are likely to be scrambling over any rocks.

For those who suffer badly from cold hands, lightweight Gore-Tex overmitts are worth considering. Added over a pair of wet ordinary running gloves they make a significant difference to hand warmth, helping ensure your fingers remain useable.

Other Things to Consider

- *Protection* – modern running kit offers plenty of alternatives to help you cope with the weather or terrain. Examples include wearing longer tights if you know you are going to be running through nettles or brambles on midsummer trail runs; selecting long white tops with a higher UPF (UV protection factor) built-in for extremely hot conditions or wearing tights and tops made from a wind-resistant material on cold and wet winter days.

- *Pockets* – there are an increasing number of tops as well as shorts and tights with pockets designed to carry MP3s and similar music players, phones, map, gels and so on – these are great if you want to use them, but additional (and sometimes unwanted) gimmicks if you do not.
- *Arm warmers* – recent years have seen an increase in the use of arm (and leg) warmers by runners. Similar to those worn by cyclists, they add another option to temperature control, in effect turning a short-sleeved top into a long one. They are therefore very useful for events where there will be significant temperature changes; for example, when going over a 2,000m pass during the night.
- *Compression garments* – compression products are now produced by all the mainstream running manufacturers, with socks and below-knee leggings being the most popular. Many claims are made about their value including reducing muscle vibration, reducing lactic acid build-up, increasing temperature control and increasing oxygen delivery to the working muscles, but few have been exposed to rigorous testing. Starting out as a recovery product, compression clothing is now increasingly worn during exercise as well. Some advocates of the below-knee socks find they reduce post-activity calf muscle soreness, while others feel they reduce cramp or calf soreness and speed up post-exercise recovery. While there is no evidence that they directly improve performance, the related effects are definitely worth considering. Similarly, as regards wearing compression bottoms for multi-day or extreme endurance events, anecdotal evidence supports their use to reduce muscle soreness and aid recovery between bouts of running or activity.

Navigational/Training Aids

Compass

By using the earth's magnetic pole, a compass helps navigation by showing the direction relative to north, south, east or west. There are plenty of different compasses on the market, all of which contain a needle that always points to the magnetic north (unless disturbed by a stronger magnetic field such as when in some parts of northern Scotland). Many GPS watches and altimeters also have a compass built into them with varying degrees of accuracy. The scope of this book does not extend to how to use a compass for navigational purposes. Readers who are not familiar with how to do so but are planning on racing where such an aid would be valuable, or just wanting to be able to explore more open terrain, would be best advised to either read further on the subject or attend a navigation course (see the section on Knowing Where You Are in Chapter 4).

When choosing a compass, the following are worth considering:

- *Size* – the larger the compass the more it weighs; the smaller it is, the more difficult the numbers will be to read.
- *Hand-held or finger* – most runners use hand-held compasses, while many orienteers prefer one designed to be attached to the finger or thumb.
- *Ease of use* – how easily does the compass housing move, particularly when you are trying to do so with cold, wet hands in gloves or mitts and it is snowing?
- *Interchangeable scale* – does it have an interchangeable scale for measuring the distance an object is away, via a map?
- *Is it quick setting?* – this refers to how quickly the needle stays stable when you are running along and following a bearing;

quick-setting compasses tend to be more expensive, but more useful if frequently changing direction and for 'fine' navigation.
- *Luminous tabs* – useful if navigating in the dark so you can see which way the needle is pointing.

Heart-Rate Monitor

A heart-rate monitor measures and displays the wearer's heart rate, displaying it in beats per minute (the number of times the heart beats and hence pumps blood around the body). This is done by wearing a chest strap, on which sensors pick up the user's heart rate and send the information to a watch-based display.

Everyone has an individually set minimum, or resting, heart rate, which tends to be lower in fitter people; and a maximum heart rate, which is largely genetically determined and falls as you get older. There is a strong correlation between how hard you are working physically and your heart rate. This is also reflected in a known relationship between heart rate and circulating blood lactate. Heart rate can, therefore, be a valuable measuring tool in training, enabling you to gauge how hard you are running and what training effect the run is having, in a non-invasive way. (It is possible to get more accurate data from measuring blood lactate, but that is somewhat impractical for most runners, involving the taking of blood from the ear lobe and sophisticated measuring equipment.)

It is possible to use normative values (or estimations) for heart rates; for example, 220 minus age is one calculation often quoted to enable people to work out their maximum heart rate; and 60–70 per cent of maximum heart rate is often quoted as equating to steady-state running pace. These, however, are very generic and of limited use to most. Much better is to undertake a fitness test at a sports-science laboratory where they will be able to provide you with accurate and individualized information to assist your training.

Altimeter

An altimeter measures and displays the altitude (or height) that the wearer is at compared with a fixed level, normally sea level. They are a very useful both to help navigate with and to record how much you have either ascended or descended. For mountain marathons and other long races, knowing the altitude you are at or how much you have climbed can be an additional help to locate a checkpoint (particularly useful in poor visibility) or gauge your effort up a hill.

Altimeters work by measuring air-pressure changes. As this is affected by the weather, when using an altimeter you should always recalibrate it against a reference feature of known height, particularly when there has been a recent weather change.

GPS

The Global Positioning System (GPS) is a navigation system based on an international network of twenty-four satellites. It provides reliable location and time information in all weathers, at all times and anywhere where there is an unobstructed line of sight to four or more satellites. GPS devices enable you to track where you have been or navigate where you are going.

One of the potential downsides of running on trails and off-road is that is it harder to accurately measure how far you have been or how fast you are running. When doing a road-based run, even prior measurement with a piece of string can give a pretty accurate measure of the distance travelled; plus, the conformity of the road surface means you are normally much better able to judge the pace you are running at, compared with off-road. A GPS watch will provide an accurate and almost instantaneous reading of distance run and speed, which is displayed on the watch as you run.

The other major benefit of a GPS watch is route recording and navigating. This can be useful, especially when you are finding your way around new trails for the first time and,

---

GPS Fix

A GPS fix is the process by which the watch synchronizes with the satellites above. It involves switching the GPS on, moving to an open, outside area and waiting until the GPS sensors in the watch have fixed with at least four satelittes, enabling an accurate position to be obtained. This can take up to twenty minutes in some areas.

For a GPS to work, it has to be fixed to at least four satellites. In heavily built-up or wooded areas, it is not uncommon for the fix to be lost or slow. We would therefore advise that when in the hills and mountains, runners never rely solely on GPS to navigate, but always have a map and compass as well. Running-focused GPS products normally take the form of a large watch, which as well as GPS-based features will also provide additional training-based functions. Top-end products now combine watch features, heart-rate data, GPS features, are compatible with bicycle-based training measurements, have an altimeter, are able to store data for downloading later to your computer, and are compatible with online mapping software.

As with heart-rate monitors, you need to be clear about what functions you want to use when researching which product to purchase, as different products have different features: some are navigationally based with more weather features, while others have a greater training focus. It is also worth remembering that technology is always advancing, products are becoming smaller, better, with more features and cheaper all the time – whatever you buy will inevitably be replaced and upgraded within twelve months.

---

for many runners, much easier than continually having to open up your map to have a look. At a basic level, a GPS unit can be set to display core navigational information such as direction and distance. Where mapping software can be uploaded, positions can then be displayed 'live' on a map on the screen, or a route pre-plotted to enable assistance with navigation.

On this last point, if you are planning to use a GPS in a race, always check that they are allowed by the race organizers. Many races that require navigational skills to be tested, forbid their use.

EQUIPMENT

Rucksack/Bum Bags

When both racing and training on the trails, it is often either required or advisable to carry extra kit/a map/food or drinks/phone and so on. Recent years have seen a big growth in the number of running-specific rucksacks and bumbags (or fanny packs) now available. Runners now have great choice as to how best to carry what they need, whether it is for a couple of hours' running on the moors or carrying mandatory kit for a 24-hour race. When deciding what to use, points to consider are:

- *Size* – how much do you need to carry? Bum bags go up to 6 litres in size, while rucksacks go from 5 litres upwards. Some runners prefer to use a bigger bum bag, others a smaller rucksack, for the same amount of gear.
- *Comfort* – does the pack sit comfortably when full and you are running, or does it bounce around? Can you get it tight enough? Do the straps rub? Does the back rub? Ideally, you should try before

you buy and do so with kit in it that you want to carry.

- *Ease of access* – can you reach what you want to reach when you need to? Most rucksacks have drinks-bottle carriers on the side or clipped on to the front. Many bumbags have bottle carriers on the back: can you easily reach the bottle (or anything else you want from a pocket) while running at reasonable speed, and then put it back once you have finished? It is much easier if you do not have to ask someone running alongside you to put your bottle back, or stop to have to do so, especially if you are racing.

- *Gear to hand* – particularly when choosing a rucksack, how many pockets do you want, either on the waistband, the top of the rucksack flap or mesh pockets on the back, so that gear or food you need to have easily available can be stored? The downside is the more pockets, the more weight – most runners prefer some pockets in order to separate items.

- *Hydration method* – do you want to use a hydration bladder or drinking bottles, or both? If you are using bottles, how many do you want? And do you want to carry them inside mesh pockets or in bottle holders on the front straps? Using bottles enables you to have different drinks with you at the same time; for example, plain water in one and an energy drink in the other.

- *Protective padding* – do you want built-in or removable padding? Many rucksacks come with a small removable sleeping mat, which can be used to sleep/sit on. Some rucksacks have padded backs – padding will, of course, increase the weight and may not be needed if you are carrying additional kit.

Rucksack or bumbag? It is a personal preference. ANDY HOLDEN

Trekking Poles

Lightweight trekking poles have become a familiar sight in continental trail races, being used by runners of all standards. They are increasingly being used in British and American races, although some race organizers do not allow their use. While many runners find them exceptionally useful, others have strong views against them. While there is little scientific evidence for the use of trekking poles while running, it is worth looking at their benefits while walking and, of course, there is plenty of anecdotal evidence (including our own) to add to the considerations.

Advantages of Poles

- *Ascending* – poles help the transfer of power from the upper body through the arms to make walking uphill easier, but whether this is real or perceived is unclear.
- *Descending* – there is some evidence that using poles can help reduce the muscle soreness associated with walking or running downhill.
- *A point of balance* – when descending poles can act as a balance point when crossing rivers or rough ground.
- *Shock absorption* – studies quoted by trekking-pole manufacturers purport to show up to 7kg less pressure per step when walking using poles and, in some cases, claim to take 25 per cent of body weight through the pole. This latter attribute is useful for those with troublesome knees or hips as it reduces the load through these joints, transferring some of it through the arms.

Disadvantages

- *Stabbing people* – anyone who has done a race in Continental Europe will appreciate the risk, especially in the early, more crowded stages of a race, of being stabbed in the leg by an over-enthusiastic runner with poles. Care also needs to be taken when taking poles out of a rucksack or putting them away, to avoid injuries to others.
- *Tripping over them* – after getting the tip stuck between rocks/in the ground.
- *Carrying them/lack of hands* – if you have poles in both or one hand, it reduces your capacity for using map and compass, getting food and drink from an aid station or eating or drinking when on the move; and, on descents, not having your arms available for balance.
- *Soreness* – the first few times you use poles be prepared to feel sore around the shoulder and upper arm muscles the next day. This is just the body getting used to a new movement.

Using poles is a very personal choice, with runners either swearing by their benefits or cursing their existence. Both authors have used poles in races and would continue do so in long European trail races where the hills tend to be longer and not as steep as those in the UK.

If you do decide to use poles or try them, there are a few things to consider when choosing which ones:

- *Weight* – it is possible to get ultra-light-weight poles made from carbon fibre or aluminium of under 250g per pair; the downside is their strength: heavier or more powerful runners may find a slightly heavier pole does not bend or break so easily.
- *Collapsible* – most runners prefer poles that can be collapsed and stored in a rucksack. The choice is between poles that are telescopic and therefore also adjustable,

or those that fold like a tent pole. The latter are non-adjustable (but will come in different lengths) but are normally also quicker and easier to extend/open or retract.

- *Pole length* – to get maximum advantage from using poles, it is important to get ones of the right height. Telescopic poles allow you to alter the pole length depending on whether you are ascending (shorter length) or descending (longer length). However, in races most runners will not bother to change pole length so as not to lose time.

- *Grip* – the grip on a trekking pole, combined with the strap, is where a lot of the power is transferred from the upper body, especially going uphill. These vary in width and length, so finding one that is comfortable is important. Some specific trail walking/running poles ('Nordic') have a special loop to facilitate this.

- *Basket* – like a ski pole, trekking poles should have a small basket at the bottom to stop the pole sinking into the mud/wet ground/snow. While on firm ground, the basket may seem a bit extraneous, trying to use poles on wet ground without one involves continually having to pull the pole out of the ground behind you, nullifying any previous advantages gained.

Head Torches

The quality of light, brightness and battery life of modern head torches means that training off-road after dark is now a very viable option for runners as well as being great fun.

Things to consider when choosing a head

Using poles to help on a long Alpine climb. AUTHORS

torch, based on what you want to use it for are:

- *Amount of light* – top-of-the-range head torches can provide the same amount of light as a standard car headlight (900–1,000 lumens), which is great if you want to cycle or run fast over really rough ground. Around 100 lumens will be enough for most on decent trails. Head torches normally have more than one light setting, with the brighter settings using the battery up faster. Also, the greater the available light, the heavier the battery tends to be.
- *Battery life* – how long do you need the head torch to be able to last on one set of batteries? Most powerful torches will give around three hours of full beam, while ones generating less power on low setting will last over 100 hours. Some torches now enable you set the amount of time you want to use it for. The torch then self-regulates the battery to provide maximum light for the set period of time, after which all light is lost.
- *Battery type* – rechargeable or single use? Rechargeable ones are great, though they tend to be a little heavier and frequently (because they come with powerful torches) do not last as long before charging is required. This means buying a spare or two if you want to use it for long periods after dark.
- *Battery position and stability* – batteries may be built into the light housing, therefore on the front of your head, attached to the back of the head band holding the light, or attached via a wire to be carried in a bum bag or rucksack or on a waistband. When deciding which product to buy, it is worth trying them out because individual runners prefer different ways of carrying the batteries. Some head-

mounted batteries have a tendency to bounce around when running, particularly the bigger ones, but some also come with an additional overhead strap to help prevent this movement.
- *Multi-use* – a number of lights come with fixings to be worn on the head or for use as a bike light.
- *Weight* – as a rough rule of thumb, the lighter the torch, the weaker the light beam; however, if you only need a head torch for emergencies, or the race regulations require you to carry a spare, then lighter is better.
- *Additional extras* – flashing lights of different colours, lights on the back of the headband, diffuser, battery-life warnings, changes to beam length and strength, tilted beam: these are some of the different options available on head torches.
- *Carrying position* – most runners wear the light on their head; however, some prefer carrying the torch or light in one hand or fastening it around the waist/chest, feeling that the lower angle results in a better depth perception for coping with uneven ground.

Modern head torches provide a significant amount of light and, when choosing which to buy, there is normally a four-way trade-off between cost, battery life, weight and brightness. In reality, as with running shoes, most runners who run or race frequently after dark end up with a range of products each best suited to different circumstances.

Hydration Systems

Whether racing or just out enjoying the hills and trails, the chances are there will be times when you need to be able to drink on the move and also to carry what you want to drink with you. This means choosing between drinking bottles or a hydration system, both of which have strengths and weaknesses.

- Traditional drinks bottles hold 500–750ml each and are typically carried in a bum bag with a pocket designed for the purpose, the mesh side pockets of a rucksack or the drinks-bottle-holder pockets on the front of a rucksack/chest harness. While many runners prefer the latter system for ease of access, others find that the bottles bounce up and down uncomfortably when running. Hand-held bottles are shaped to fit over your hand and be held continuously while running. They typically hold less fluid (200–500ml) and are relatively easy to use while on the run and to refill. The obvious downside is running with the weight in your hand plus the hand now being full, when it might also be needed to clamber over rocks, get over stiles, or hold a map and compass. You can also get hand-held bottle straps, which enable you to hold an ordinary drinks bottle in your hand.

- It is possible to get both rucksacks and bum bags that take hydration bladders, and many runners prefer these to the more traditional bottles as they can sip from the drinking tube as they run along. The downside is that they are not as easy or as quick to refill as a bottle during a race and, while they can carry more fluid to start with, the more you have, the more weight you carry.

Whichever system you find works best for you, always remember to clean the inside of the drinking container thoroughly, as this is a place notorious for the potential to grow mould.

CHAPTER 6

LOOKING AFTER YOUR BODY

The best way to become a better runner is to run. However, all runners can maximize their enjoyment of running and become better runners if they also look after themselves both physically and mentally.

Injury, illness, doing too much (or having too little recovery), eating and drinking poorly: these are all common detractors from performance and the enjoyment of running. Here, of course, trail, mountain and fell runners are no different from any other runner. There are, however, injuries (such as twisted ankles) and illnesses (such as Lyme disease) that are more common among those who run on trails and mountains. Although all injuries cannot be prevented, awareness of the causes of injury, as well as working on your own known weaknesses, can help reduce them.

Injuries

Overuse Injuries

Overuse/chronic injuries are caused by 'over-loading' a particular part of the body, either in quantity or quality and are generally the result of doing 'too much' hard running or suddenly introducing too much of something new. Too much is, however, different for everyone and needs to be calibrated against what your body is used to. A crude rule, often quoted, is not to increase your training load by more than 10 per cent per week. Obviously, there is a limit to this and hence 'periodization' and

careful planning of training and racing are important (see Chapters 1 and 2 for more on training). Not only do you need to take into account previous training history, but also the individualization principle, which means that different people tolerate different workloads.

It is always important to adjust your training to suit your body and not get worried or try to copy what others do. With experience, most runners learn to 'listen to their body' and know when they can 'up' their training or should ease off. The key point to mention here is age or, more specifically, training age (that is, the number of years' training you have done as opposed to how old you are); it is a rare older athlete who is able either to recover as fast after injury/hard training or to cope with the same training load as they could ten years previously. For example, in her early training years, SR was able to manage a reasonably high mileage (c.90–100 miles a week), as well as handle back-to-back hard training days without breaking down. She was able to do 18–20-mile runs even after a period of lay-off without ill effect. One of her training contemporaries of the time, an athlete of similar ability in terms of race performances, but more of a speed-focused athlete, not only required longer to recover from a hard speed session, but also would always need to build up the length of her long runs slowly in order to avoid injury.

Of course, as far as SR is concerned, much of this has changed with age, and while the long runs remain possible off little training, any long or hard days have to be followed by at least two or three easy ones to minimize the risk of injury.

Recording 'Niggles'

Being able to track and keep a record of small aches and niggles is one of the most valuable aspects of keeping a training log. Recording after each run which bits hurt or ached and how badly or for how long, will provide you with a valuable record by which to track and keep an eye on little niggles, so that you can seek treatment before they become major problems. By being able to look back at the training you did in the weeks leading up to developing a chronic symptom, it may also be possible to see what training/racing may have caused it.

Generally, trail, mountain and fell running is less likely to lead to major chronic problems such as stress fractures and shin splints compared with road running. This is because the overall force going through the lower body in a consistent manner is less, due to two factors: first, when running on an even surface such as tarmac or even very flat and smooth paths, the direction of force (and hence loading) through the legs is constant with every stride; second, the reaction force through the leg from the impact of the foot hitting the ground is greater from tarmac (Newton's third law of motion states that every action produces equal and opposite reaction), and if the loading is excessive, it can be a contributing factor to chronic or overuse injury. Off-road, not only is the reaction transmitted through the leg and body less than from road, whether on grass or hard-packed trail, it is also in a continually changing pattern of stride length and foot position as you adapt to the variations of the terrain, so there is continual – if at times minute – change in the loading pattern of the lower body.

Acute Injuries

While overuse injuries as a rule are less common in trail, mountain and fell runners, acute injuries resulting from an unexpected twist or turn, when the body is not quick enough to correct, are more common. With training, the body becomes better accustomed to coping with the ever-changing demands of uneven ground and, with improvement in balance, these types of injuries are less likely to occur. Vigilance is, however, always required, particularly when fatigue sets in. Bizarrely, trips and falls often happen when coming to the end of a particularly steep or rocky piece of ground when you relax your concentration just a little too much. SR had one such fall towards the end of the Ben Nevis Race one year when, having successfully negotiated the rougher terrain, she switched her focus too much to chasing down a male runner in front of her – the result was a hefty fall, causing badly bruised hands, knees and ego.

Sprained Ankle

Of all sporting injuries, and in trail, mountain and fell running in particular, ankle sprains are the most common and can vary from mild, when the runner is able to continue, through varying degrees of severity. Acute injuries are caused when the sudden force going through a soft tissue is too great for the soft-tissue structure, causing it to tear, completely or in part. When an ankle is sprained ('going over' on an ankle), usually on the outer (or lateral) side, the ligaments supporting the ankle are stretched and some fibres of the ligament may be torn. In addition, there is damage to small blood vessels in the stretched tissue, which causes bleeding and later bruising, with subsequent swelling. It is important to relieve pain and maintain ankle movement (see below).

Strong ankles are needed to run off-road. TRISS KENNY

Minimize Acute Injuries

To help avoid acute injuries, balance becomes more important off-road, and specific exercises (such as those given in Chapter 3) can help you prepare for this. By training over rough ground, your body becomes more adept at dealing with an unexpected foot plant. On known terrain, familiarity is helpful. Thus, walking or running at sub-race pace over a race course prior to the event allows you to gain visual and body familiarity with awkward, technical sections underfoot: rocks, tree roots, loose scree and so on. This allows you to be prepared for conditions on race day (and, of course, helps you make the right choice of race footwear).

When WD needed to compete in the Kentmere Horseshoe Race as part of the English Championship series, she had to do so two weeks after having had a plate put into

her shoulder to repair a broken collarbone. A week before the race, she purposely went over the whole course (at walking pace) checking out all the tricky sections so that she could, on race day, choose a route that minimized the risk of a fall, particularly on wet and slippery rocks. While on this occasion all went well, racing with a freshly broken collarbone is perhaps not to be recommended, though she had watched another championship race two weeks earlier, before the broken bone was plated!

As a trail, mountain and fell runner, it is worth having a good understanding of your relative strengths and weaknesses over rough ground and then adapt your race tactics accordingly; for example, in races like the Ben Nevis, many runners will go as hard as possible on the ascent to make up time as they know that the very rough technical descent will require caution and concentration and a slower than optimal descent pace to reduce the very real risk of falling or twisting something. Conversely, those runners who excel on rough technical descents tend to take it a little easier on the climb, keeping their legs relatively fresh, knowing that they will then go at full blast on the descent and will catch those being more cautious. Likewise, if you are 'blindly' following another runner while running in thick mist, you want to be sure that you are relatively as good as them should the terrain become more technical; otherwise, despite your best efforts you will be left behind.

Injury Treatment

Acute Soft-Tissue Injuries

Using an ankle sprain as an example, the following describes the basic first-aid principles that should be used for all acute soft tissue (as opposed to bony) injuries. The important thing is to remember and apply (**PR**)**ICE**, the key part being **ICE**, as soon as possible:

- **I**ce or cold should be applied to the damaged area as soon as possible, the aim being to reduce the amount of bleeding from damaged tissues. This could be in the form of plunging it into a nearby stream, obtaining ice from the bar in a nearby pub or using a packet of frozen peas (or similar) on your return home. To avoid ice burn, any ice or frozen packets should be wrapped in a damp cloth or towel before applying it to the skin. The cold should be kept in place for ten minutes and repeated several times daily in the first few days. Cold also provides some pain relief.
- **C**ompression following cold or ice application serves to reduce the amount of swelling in the ankle, which is desirable as swelling will restrict movement. This can

be obtained with firm tape (assuming that you are not sensitive to the adhesive in the tape) or by using an elasticated bandage. Make sure that you do not apply this too tightly or it will result in restricted blood flow to the rest of the foot.

- **E**levation of the ankle, ideally above waist height, further helps to reduce the amount of swelling. The same principle is applicable to most acute injuries, modifying as appropriate to the affected body part and location.
- The **'P'** of **PRICE** stands for protection, which means protecting the injured area if necessary – for example, by strapping in the case of an ankle sprain – to avoid further injury/damage.
- The **'R'** stands for rest or, more specifically, relative rest from any activity that will further damage the ankle or inhibit the healing process. For an injury that prevents immediate return to running, alternative forms of exercise should be considered. The aim is to maintain cardiovascular (aerobic) fitness and keep the major muscles in the legs moving. Thus, cycling, running in water and swimming (as mentioned in Chapter 10) can all potentially be used.

After the immediacy of the first couple of hours, the less the swelling is, the easier movement will be, and hence the importance of reducing bleeding and swelling in the area. As soon as pain allows, you should start walking within the limits of pain. An ankle sprain that results in having to stop or retire from a race can take anything from a few days to weeks for full recovery to occur, depending on the severity. The only major difference in the composition of ligaments that are damaged in an ankle sprain and a broken bone is the presence of calcium in the latter, so severe sprains must be treated with respect when bone bruising might also be present. When walking is comfortable, then easy running can be started, again within the limits of pain.

If there is a delay in being able to run again, then the muscles will rapidly weaken around any injured joint and positive action should be taken to counteract this and to restore range of motion. Here, a physiotherapist should be able to advise on key exercises you should do.

Particularly important after an ankle injury is to re-educate your balance mechanisms and restore kinaesthetic/proprioceptive function (the ability to know the position of a body part). This can be done as described in the section on Balance in Chapter 3, or may require more sophisticated exercises based

Using a river for some natural post-race cooling. ANDY HOLDEN

on the advice of a physiotherapist. In order to reduce risk of re-injury, you need to ensure ankle strength, proprioception and range of motion are all restored to optimum levels.

Some off-road runners tape their ankles as a matter of course when racing and even training, to minimize injury risk. This is usually done after an earlier injury, which may have resulted in a functionally unstable ankle (an anatomically unstable ankle being rare when compared with the knee where, after a significant ligament injury, the joint is liable to 'give way' on account of anatomical instability). While this may be fine in the short term, in the long run it is much better to strengthen the muscles supporting the ankle and work at balance exercises, than continually rely on taping to prevent further injury.

Muscle Injuries

Acute muscle injuries are common in all types of runners, but perhaps most commonly in sprinters when there is a sudden burst of power, which puts maximum stress through certain leg muscles. A strained or 'pulled' muscle requires the same basic first aid of **ICE**. This should then be followed as soon as possible with initial gentle stretching, the aim being to stretch out the 'pulled' segment of muscle so that it stretches to the same extent as the surrounding muscle when healed. The alternative is a shorter section of muscle and a significant risk of it being 'pulled' next time force is applied, and chronicity may ensue (when what started as an acute muscle tear becomes a long-term chronic problem). The aim following a muscle injury is to ensure that the damaged area is as extensible (stretches as much) as the uninjured muscle and is of equal strength. Subsequent weakness should only occur if the injury is severe and limits activity for any significant time. The same treatment applies

when a muscle is injured by a direct blow, which, for a trail, mountain and fell runner may occur when falling on rock.

Medication

Whether to use medication for pain relief is controversial. Painkillers, such as paracetamol, for comfort are a personal choice, depending on the amount of pain. Non-steroidal anti-inflammatory tablets such as ibuprofen undoubtedly make an injury more comfortable. There are theoretical reasons that they may affect healing but this has never been experimentally proven so, again, it is an individual decision. Apart from recognized side effects, such as on the stomach, there is no evidence that they cause harm when taken for an injury in the correct dose.

Current good practice as recommended by physiotherapists is to not take anti-inflammatory tablets in the first 48–72hr after an acute soft-tissue injury. This is to let the body's natural healing process work. For this reason, unless there was a large amount of swelling that you might want to limit, paracetamol is a good way to reduce pain. Do not take aspirin as it can increase bleeding and therefore adversely affect healing times.

Massage

Massage is another controversial subject and one where there is limited scientific evidence to fully support its use in terms of improving performance or reducing injury. Generally, it makes the runner feel better and can reduce muscle soreness, and probably in doing so has a psychological benefit. Where perhaps it can be most beneficial is when used as a therapeutic treatment for tight, knotted or tethered (stuck together not gliding across each other) soft tissues; something that tends to be pretty painful but with positive outcomes in terms of future ability to run smoothly.

Getting the Best from a Physiotherapist

Both authors have had cause to use or work with physiotherapists and what follows are things that we would take into account when choosing and using a physiotherapist.

Choosing
- What are their qualifications? If they are practising as a physiotherapist they must be a member of the Chartered Society of Physiotherapy (CSP) and be Health Professions Council (HPC) registered.
- Do they have experience or qualifications that relate to sporting and, in particular, running injuries?
- Do you know someone who has been treated by them or recommends them? Physiotherapists are governed by what they can say in public adverts; the best recommendation is often word of mouth.
- Conversely, remember every patient is different, and even the best physiotherapists worldwide will have had athletes whom they have struggled to help, so do not be put off by one poor story.
- Do they treat your injury problem or its cause? There are numerous causes of, say, an inflamed Achilles tendon, and just treating the tendon itself will not provide a long-term solution. The cause of the inflammation, which may be linked to another part of the body, needs to be identified and solved – perhaps the one skill that distinguishes a world-class physiotherapist from a good one.
- Is the physiotherapist prepared to refer you on or seek additional advice if your injury proves difficult to sort out? Most injuries should respond reasonably quickly to the right treatment, so if you have been going to the same physiotherapist for three to four months with the same problem, is it time to seek a second opinion?
- Depending on the injury, do they treat manually or just use machines? Current best practice within physiotherapy is for a much greater use of manual therapy rather than simply blasting the site with some sort of electronic device. If, following the concept that the sore area may be caused by issues elsewhere (alignment), it may be that the acutely injured area needs electrotherapy, but the issues that have caused the injury need to be treated at the same time to help prevent recurrence.

Using
- Do not expect a miracle cure within one treatment session; do, however, on your first visit, ask the physiotherapist how long/how many treatments they think you will need. If your injury is still not better after this block of treatment, get an update from them and ask if a referral to another health professional might be worth considering.
- Be honest with them: tell them the truth about what exercise you have been doing and are doing – only if the physiotherapist knows the true picture can they help you.
- Agree with them what exercise (whether running, gym or cross-training) you can do, and stick to it; your physiotherapist will want to get you back running, will know you want to run and will advise you accordingly. Doing more than they recommend is only likely to prolong your period of treatment, delay full recovery and cost you more.
- Do the rehabilitation exercises they recommend; look on them as training, and keep doing them (or a shorter, less intense version) once the original problem has eased, as this will help prevent injury recurrence.
- Finally, do not think of a physiotherapist just as someone who treats injuries, they are also great for helping prevent them in the first place. Most top runners will have regular check-ups with their physiotherapist to make sure everything is in line, in balance, and the body strong enough for the task asked of it when running. While no longer a top runner, SR knows that with a period of sustained and long training, especially if it is cold, one of her ankles stiffens badly and, in effect, locks up. Although the change is unnoticeable to her as it happens gradually, past experience means a check-up every one to two months keeps this potential injury cause, and others, in check (well, most of the time!).

Other Medical Issues

Cramp

Cramp is an enigma. From a purely physiological perspective, it is a muscle going into spasm. There is no doubt that it is more troublesome with increasing age. The spasm that is cramp would appear to be related to increased excitability of the muscle fibres, but exactly why this should occur is unclear. It is more common when there is high ambient temperature with large fluid losses, with prolonged exercise and if different types of exercises have been undertaken. For example, it is more likely to occur when swimming if this follows on from a hard long run. The commonest site for cramp in runners is the calf, but it can occur in any muscle, including the abdominal muscles, such as when a lot of 'double poling' is undertaken in ultra-distance cross-country ski races.

By ensuring adequate hydration and electrolyte replacement, hot-weather cramp may be minimized. Likewise, there is some association between a higher salt/electrolyte intake and/or taking salt/electrolyte replacement tablets and a reduction in the occurrence of cramp, especially during hot, long races or similar.

Older people may get spontaneous cramp in bed at night and, although the condition is the same – a muscle spasm – it is not exercise related. Quinine has been used for these night cramps but there is no significant evidence that it has any definite effect.

Management of cramp involves trying to stretch the offending muscle, which as everyone knows who has suffered mid-race from cramp, is easier said than done. This is not only difficult but as painful as the cramp itself. Ideally it is best to learn to stretch the muscle out yourself, but if this is not possible, find a friend. The surprising thing about cramp is that it can be 'got through', even if the initial cramp brings you to a complete halt.

Under-Recovery or Overtraining

Optimal training for performance is a fine balance for all athletes: train too little and you do not improve as much as you could; train too much and you risk injury or illness, or suffering what is known as under-recovery syndrome (this is also often referred to as overtraining syndrome). And herein lies the real art of coaching or getting your own performances right. The optimal training programme is one that puts a greater stress on the body than it is used to, so bringing about positive adaptations, but not one so great that you do not recover properly. Getting the balance right is a very fine line. As an athlete, you are used to feeling tired and at times being able to continue to run when tired. However, when you become overtired or under-recovered, trying to run and train through it is the worst thing you can do (as SR knows to her cost). Rather, it is time to ease right off and allow your body to recover mentally and physically.

What, then, are the signs of under-recovery and how do they differ from the natural tiredness experienced after a hard training session or race? Unfortunately, at the time of writing, while there are a number of signs and symptoms that runners can monitor, there is no one guaranteed gold-standard test that will either indicate that you are not recovering well or that you have crossed the fine line between training tiredness and having overtrained. Such a test remains something that medical and scientific experts continue to try to find. Part of the problem is that, while there are numerous theories, it is not yet fully clear what causes under-recovery symptom or, as it is often known, Unexplained Underperformance Syndrome (UPS). The current view is that there is no one single cause of UPS; rather that there are a whole host of potential influencing factors, as well as different ways that UPS subsequently manifests itself.

Perhaps the best way of thinking about this is as a stress balance, whereby UPS occurs when an individual runner's overall stress capacity becomes overloaded and the body is unable to recover. While this stress is often related to the amount and type of training carried out, you cannot ignore the other forms of stress – work, personal, social, family – that may also be going on in your life.

SR experienced a bout of UPS in the late 1980s, one which with hindsight and current knowledge could have been avoided. After an operation on her leg, she had just built back up to her normal training volume (then 80–90 miles per week) and, over a period of a couple of months, was racing most weekends. This in itself would not have been a problem, as it was within the normal stress levels she was used to handling. At the time, however, she had recently bought a flat, moved to Eastbourne and had just started her PhD, the sum total of which was a stress overload.

Key, therefore, to avoiding UPS or overtraining is not only careful planning of training and racing (if you have had three or four great weeks' training, perhaps it is time to ease back a bit for a few days), but also reviewing what else is going on in your life. If you are having a stressful time at work, for example, think about either reducing the volume or quality of your training, so that at a time when work is a greater stressor, your running is more of a stress reducer.

Another way of looking at it is: if you add something to your training, then you should also look to take something out, hence keeping the overall effort in balance. A very good way of keeping an eye on this, and one

that can also help provide you with a true record of how you feel and what training you have been doing, is by keeping a training diary. By regularly recording your daily training plus how you feel both running and in general (for example, hours slept, general mood, morning pulse, weight), you can easily look back and see that the 'general feeling of tiredness and poor sessions' have been going on for three to four weeks and that proper rest is called for.

As with everything, how well you recover from hard training sessions and races is quite individual; some runners may be back in a normal training routine the day after a race, while others need two or three recovery days (or longer for longer races). Preventing overtraining is about being able to read your own body and notice that you are not recovering as you should, that the feeling of heavy legs and of plodding rather than running does not go away after a couple of easy days and that you are feeling low and depressed and not sleeping well.

Accepting that you are not superhuman and that your body is telling you it needs longer to rest and recover is key when this happens. If you are lucky and you read the signs early, you should find that a week of much reduced running or complete rest is enough to get you back on track. In true cases of UPS, a period of up to 6–12 weeks of rest with no more than very light alternative exercise, starting with no more than 5–10min a day and building up slowly, is recommended. After this you should be able to gradually build back up to previous levels of training. If you are ever unfortunate enough to find yourself in this position, you should always check with your GP first and ask for a blood test to ensure that nothing else is wrong or contributing to your lethargy; for example, low iron or magnesium levels or an underactive thyroid gland.

> ## Warning Signs of Under-Recovery or Overtraining
>
> Increased morning resting pulse (up to ten beats per minute)
>
> Disturbed or poor sleep despite feeling tired
>
> Feeling depressed and irritable
>
> Frequent and longer bouts of minor infections
>
> Loss of weight and or appetite
>
> Loss of libido
>
> Increased tiredness during training, plus a greater sense of effort for the speed run at, which does not decline after a couple of easy days
>
> Heavy, stiff and sore muscles
>
> Inability to raise your heart rate during attempted hard training sessions
>
> Sudden drop in performance
>
> Reduced ability to concentrate

Tick-Borne Diseases

One area that road runners rarely have to worry about, but which can be an issue for those who run in wilder places, is that of tick-borne diseases. These have been around for a long time, and walkers and orienteers in Hungary and Austria have been particularly at risk of tick-borne encephalitis, with immunization advised if you are likely to be in high-risk areas such as woods or forests. Lyme disease is the tick-borne disease that can cause problems to mountain, trail and fell runners and other outdoor enthusiasts in the UK, Europe and America. Sheep and deer ticks can carry the spirochaete, *Borrelia burgdorferi*, which causes Lyme disease. If an infected tick feeds on a secondary host such as a human, then there is a risk of contracting this disease. The longer the contact with an infected tick (the longer it is attached to your skin), the greater the risk of the disease developing. Ticks are particularly prevalent in the Highlands of Scotland, Galloway and the New Forest but are increasingly present in the Lake District.

Essentially, wherever there are deer and sheep, ticks are about. It is therefore very important to do a self- or friend-check for ticks, particularly between April and October, if you have been running through long grass or bracken with bare arms or legs. If you run with a dog, then you should also check it for ticks on a regular basis, though there is no evidence of a tick passing from a dog to a human.

As a word of warning, ticks are very good at getting into small crevices, and wearing tight Lycra shorts, as opposed to traditional running ones, in known tick-infested areas has the added advantage of keeping your groin region (male and female) well protected from potential invaders. Our known record for ticks removed from one person is fifty-eight – this was from an individual with a reasonable amount of body hair after a two-day mountain marathon in Scotland – and some of them were in pretty intimate places; on which note, using a mirror or getting a friend to check your backside should also be considered.

To remove a tick, either use a tick remover (available from most veterinary practices), or use a pair of tweezers, and gently rotate the body of the tick that you have firmly grasped in the tweezers, until the mouth parts let go of the skin – it is important to make sure that the whole of the tick has been removed and not just the body. There is no truth in the rumour that you must rotate clockwise. Other tried and tested methods of tick removal are smothering them in petroleum jelly so that they suffocate and drop off or burning them with a match, though the latter is best avoided on those with a significant amount of body hair!

If you get Lyme disease, you may get a characteristic skin rash, flu-like symptoms, joint pains or nerve difficulties. If you suspect that you have been infected, you should visit your GP as soon as possible as a course of antibiotics can cure the disease, especially if treated in its early stages. However, late diagnosis can lead to more serious symptoms and a less effective cure as some permanent physical changes may have occurred.

In Eastern Europe and parts of Scandinavia, there is the risk of tick-borne encephalitis (TBE). There is preventative immunization against this so, if competing there, it is worth checking whether there is a risk by looking at the website www.tickalert.org.

Weil's disease is another condition caused by a spirochaete, *Leptospira interogans*, but is not tick-borne and is likely to be picked up only if going through water contaminated with rat urine, so is more of a risk for water-sports enthusiasts rather than trail, mountain and fell runners.

Classic tick country. ANDY HOLDEN

Nutrition

In this section, we outline the core basics of a good nutrition plan for trail, mountain and fell runners, which in reality is no different to that for any endurance runner. Chapters 7, 8 and 9 cover in more detail what and when to eat and drink before, during and after racing, while the use of legal ergogenic aids or supplements are covered in Chapter 11. For those wanting to know more on this topic, there are plenty of books and articles devoted to food and fluid intake for runners and other athletes, including those listed at the end of this section.

Food

Despite what many would have you believe, eating optimally for performance is not greatly different from eating optimally for health. Yes, there are some differences: for example, runners will have a greater need for energy and, in particular, carbohydrate, a slightly higher protein requirement for muscle repair, potentially less need for high-fibre products and a greater leniency for occasional energy-dense/lower-nutritional-value foods. In a similar vein, there are no miracle foods, pills, drinks or supplements that will make you a better runner. In the same way that poor training and lifestyle habits will have an adverse effect on your running, so will poor nutritional ones. Optimal nutrition, on the other hand, will help ensure that you maximize your potential, but cannot make you better than that.

What does the term optimal nutrition mean in real life? First, it should be remembered that there are no 'bad' foods; namely, foods that – in moderation and as part of an overall well-balanced diet – will have an adverse effect on performance (allergies and intolerances aside). This point is very important because food, for most people, is not just something that we eat to sustain life, it is something that has significant social and psychological meaning to us. We eat to enjoy, our social lives often include eating and drinking and most of us derive great pleasure from what we eat. As was once said by a well-known Olympic coach: 'the process of being an elite athlete is a dehumanising one', meaning that much of what athletes at this level have to do in terms of what they eat and drink and the lifestyle they live, when not training, goes against the normal human social niceties.

For most runners, such an approach is not only unrealistic, it is also unacceptable in terms of their wider life happiness. Quoting Charlie Spedding, the British runner who won the bronze medal in the 1984 Olympic Games marathon and had a personal best of 2hr 08.33sec for the event: 'I give up so much of my life to be a good runner and train hard; having a beer in the evening is one pleasure I keep.'

Much better, and more easily sustainable in the long term, is the pragmatic approach. Ensure that you have a varied diet, which:

- In energy terms, is made up of at least 50 per cent carbohydrate (or 8–10g per kg body weight), with 10–25 per cent fat and 10–25 per cent protein.
- Contains all the essential nutrients (amino acids, vitamins, minerals) in amounts that meet your requirements – all runners, but particularly female ones, should make sure that they include enough good sources of iron and calcium in their diets.
- Has at least five portions of fruit or vegetables a day.
- Includes no more than moderate amounts of alcohol; there is no evidence that moderate amounts of alcohol impair performance, especially among runners who are regular moderate drinkers. Those wanting to lose weight should limit alcohol

intake to avoid 'empty' calories, while post-race or training you should make sure that you have rehydrated and refuelled before you start on the beer.
- Balances energy intake with energy output (unless you are trying to either gain or lose weight).
- If vegetarian or vegan, includes enough quality sources of B vitamins and all the essential amino acids.
- Does not depend too heavily on 'junk' or low-quality highly processed foods.
- Is based around what works for you and what you like.

There are some areas where a runner's diet often veers away from what may be called a 'healthy' diet, in particular:

- The inclusion of some sugary drinks and energy-dense but nutritionally 'light' products, such as sweets, chocolates and so on – runners will by default need to eat more than sedentary people, often requiring upwards of an extra 1,000-plus kcal per day to fuel their training. Getting 10 or even 20 per cent of this extra energy from so-called junk foods is not a problem if the rest of your diet is sound.
- The use of wholegrain and high-fibre-based products is recommended to help maintain good gut health. From a practical point of view, too much of this combined with running can often lead to feeling bloated when training or inconvenient bouts of runner's trots.
- Taking a multi-vitamin and mineral supplement 'just in case'. There is no scientific evidence to support excessive intakes of any vitamins or minerals; however, taking a balanced multi-vitamin and mineral supplement as an insurance will not harm you either and is often the preferred option, if only for peace of mind.

Fluid

There has recently been a trend towards encouraging everyone to drink more, with water fountains now found in most offices, and people carrying water bottles as they go about their daily routine a common sight. As with most trends, there is, at the time of writing, the first signs that this push to drink more is being questioned, with the current NHS advice to drink six to eight glasses of water (or other fluids) a day being challenged in the *British Medical Journal* (July 2011).

Take the same issue and add in exercise, and the sides of the debate get more heated. On the one hand, humans are evolved from hunter-gatherers and therefore have developed to be able to cope with long periods in the heat without too much fluid (something often cited when referring to the apparent low fluid intakes of Kenyan marathon runners either in racing or training). This is combined with the fact that overdrinking in races, particularly if the drink has a low level of electrolyte present, can lead to hyponatraemia (low sodium). On the other side of the argument are the oft-quoted studies that show a decline in performance if the body is dehydrated by more than 2–3 per cent of body weight.

In truth, the answer is probably somewhere in the middle: drinking and keeping ourselves hydrated is important as we can survive for quite some time without food but only a few days without water. However, the recent push, especially among runners, to drink lots and frequently, is now recognized as having been excessive. A good example of this is from a marathon training camp that SR was involved with. Taking place in March, the runners assembled for a pre-breakfast 5km run on the first morning in wet and drizzly weather. It was somewhat of a surprise to see at least two of the runners arrive complete with water bottle to take and drink from en route – in those ambient conditions it was not needed, nor possible, to become dehydrated.

Some Thoughts on Drinking

- If you are 'peeing' plenty of straw-coloured urine, the chances are that you are fully hydrated. Small amounts of dark urine mean more fluid is required.
- For training runs of up to 2hr in the UK, unless the temperature is very high, you should be fine drinking plenty before and on your return from your run; longer runs, especially in the summer, will require taking fluid with you, or picking it up en route.
- When training, fluid intake should aim to prevent significant weight loss from fluid loss – you can easily work out how much sweat you lose on a run by weighing yourself dry and naked before and after a run.
- There is considerable variability in both individual sweat rates and sweat composition; ideally, therefore, you should develop your own personal drinking plan.
- When you are heat acclimatized you produce more sweat, which is more dilute. High sweaters can lose up to 2 litres of sweat per hour (this equates to 2kg of weight loss).
- Post-exercise, fluid should be replaced by drinking 1.5 times the amount of fluid lost and should be consumed alongside sodium, either in food or within the drink, as this will help fluid absorption.
- In the UK, if high in the hills, it is generally safe to drink water from rapidly flowing streams, ideally above the 'sheep line' to avoid risk of contamination from animal excretion. Drinking still water and water at lower levels is always a risk, so when in doubt 'don't'. The authors have never come to harm over many years of drinking

from mountain streams (in the UK), though always look upstream to ensure that no dead sheep, or worse, is lying there! Sterilizing tablets can be used to be absolutely sure, particularly if at low levels or in heavily farmed areas. In warmer climates, it is not a good idea to drink stream water.

- Similar principles apply to personal hygiene – after falling in mud and worse, be sensible about feeding and take any opportunity to clean muddy hands before filling up on your next energy 'fix'.
- If you are trying to lose weight, remember that sports drinks, unless they are the low-calorie variety, contain energy, often as much as a can of fizzy drink, and should therefore be used sparingly.

- Caffeine and alcohol are both diuretics, namely, they stimulate urine output, resulting in less fluid being absorbed into the bloodstream. Habitual caffeine drinking does not, however, seem to adversely affect hydration status.

Recommended reading:

Fluid guidelines: American College of Sports Medicine, Feb. 2007. Exercise and Fluid Replacement. *Medicine & Science in Sports & Exercise*, vol. I, issue 2, pp. 377–390 (http://journals.lww.com/acsm-msse)

Griffin, Jane, 2005. *Nutrition for Marathon Running*. The Crowood Press (ISBN 978 1 86126 590 6: e-book ISBN 978 1 84797 405 1)

PART II

RACING

The first part of the book covered the training fundamentals, things of use to any and everyone who runs. This next section focuses much more on racing, examining best practice for pre-race preparation, the race itself and post-race recovery for each of our hypothetical races.

The UTMB 2011, Jez Bragg on the Col de la Seigne. THE NORTH FACE

CHAPTER *7*

PRE-RACE PREPARATION

Having a good race performance is not just about putting in all the hard training, especially with trail-, mountain-, and fell-running races where there are so many other elements that come into play. In this chapter, we explore further the critical areas that you need to think about as you prepare specifically for your planned race, in each case showing how or what you do varies depending on the type of race you are training for.

Getting your pre-race non running preparation right is vital and can make all the difference between having a great run and a poor one, or – even worse – not finishing due to basic errors such as going the wrong way, not having enough food or drink, or wearing the wrong shoes.

First, here is a reminder of our four hypothetical races:

A 45min fell race A typical British fell race: going to the top of a steep hill and back down, where there is off-path running; the race route is unmarked; runners can choose their own route.

A 90min mountain race A traditional European mountain race, which is primarily uphill on a fully marked course.

A 3hr trail race On a mix of undulating trails, grasslands, paths, bits of roads; the race checkpoints must be visited, maybe marked; some support provided en route.

A 10hr-plus ultra race On a mix of undulating trails/grasslands, paths, roads; the race route must be followed but it is not marked; some support en route provided at the checkpoints; the main difference from the trail race is duration.

Pre-Race Training Considerations

Chapter 2 gave examples of typical training programmes for each of the four races. Given below are some additional points that you should take into account when planning your training programme; in particular, the types of surfaces that you should be training on, including, at times, for faster-based work. There is no point doing all your speed work on flat, smooth surfaces if you then need to race over undulating tussocks.

A 45min Fell Race

- Will be over rough ground, requiring strong, stable ankle joints and an ability to chop and change as you adapt your stride while moving fast, especially coming downhill – some fast running should be done in training over similar terrain.
- Going uphill over rough ground often means fast walking.
- Paths are likely to be very narrow in places, making overtaking difficult and requiring sudden bursts of speed, which are also needed for getting to the front of a group approaching any stiles or gates en route. Training sessions should therefore take this into account.

A 90min Mountain Race

- It is likely to be at least partly on good paths, so you need to develop your base speed.
- Courses are also often at least partly on loose shale four-wheel-drive tracks or wooded paths with rocks and roots. The former mean it is difficult at times to get solid traction with the ground; the latter requires you to adjust your stride and disrupt your rhythm, so practising running fast over similar terrain is important.
- The steepness may vary from quite flat to up to a 15–20 per cent gradient. In really steep races, even the top runners will use bouts of fast walking, which will often be quicker than slow running as well as giving a slight respite due to using different muscle groups – again, something to practise in training.
- Cycling is excellent for developing the muscles used for climbing, and sessions on the bike can be used in addition or instead of some running ones.
- Exercises to strengthen your calf, gluteal and hamstring muscles will help prevent local muscle fatigue (see the specific strengthening exercises in Chapter 3).

A 3hr Trail Race

- Performances will be boosted by taking fluid and fuel during the race; this should be practised during your long training runs.
- Even good trails frequently require you to adjust your stride, so practising running at race pace or faster on similar surfaces is important.
- For many runners, periods of fast walking on the steeper parts may be quicker than slow running.

A 10hr-Plus Ultra Race

- Race pace will most likely be slower than normal steady training pace and should be practised in training, including incorporating bouts of walking.
- A race of this length, while still very physiologically demanding, requires great mental strength: it is often about who can mentally handle the distance and 'bad' patches the best.
- Time on your feet in training is important, building up to being able to cover 30 miles in one go, mixing running and walking.
- Even good trails frequently require you to adjust your stride and disrupt your rhythm, so practise running at slightly faster than race pace on similar surfaces.
- Practise running with the kit you will need to take on race day to make sure you do not suffer from rubbing – as happened to SR 1hr into a race that was going to last over 30hr; luckily, she was carrying zinc oxide tape with her and was able to stop and quickly tape the offending part.
- Periods of walking, particularly on the steeper parts, will be quicker than slow running as well as giving a slight respite due to using different muscle groups.
- Eating and drinking en route will be essential; again, practise in training; races of this length are sometimes won or lost depending on who best manages their fuel intake.

Race Homework

Runners moving to trails and mountains from road and cross-country racing will be used to doing a bit of pre-race homework: checking out where the start is, how far away parking is, where race registration is, having a look at the map of the course and thinking about what to wear. Much of this is the same for trail, mountain and fell races, but with a few added twists unique to this branch of the sport.

Directions/Instructions

As with any race or event, make sure that you have read the race instructions well beforehand. Longer races will often have detailed kit and equipment lists (do not simply rely on knowing what was needed last year as things frequently change, particularly with longer events), as well as race 'road books' with instructions about route choice, rules, what is and is not allowed from supporters and so on. Reading this well in advance gives you plenty of time to make sure you have everything planned as well as the right kit. For example, SR did a point-to-point 50-mile race, which started at midday. Her notional plan was to drive to the start with her supporter, register an hour beforehand, after which her supporter would drive the car to the end of the race. Race instructions, however, required registration at the event HQ, which was at the end of the race, not at the start point, with a bus taking competitors to the start – something SR found out on careful reading of the details a week beforehand, which in all truthfulness was on the late side.

Reconnoitre

Reconnoitring a race route, or part of one, is common practice for cross-country races (where it can easily be done as part of the pre-race warm-up). Other than checking out the finish run-in, doing so is less common for road races. For trail, mountain and fell-running events, a 'recce' can be very useful and, particularly among fell and ultra runners, is common practice, assuming always that the race route is on public rather than private land.

Depending on the nature of the event, the focus of the reconnoitre, other than getting a good feel for what the course is like underfoot and in topographical profile, will differ.

A 45min Fell Race

Even a 45min unmarked fell race has the potential to provide plenty of opportunity for route choice and, particularly if the mist is down, going wrong. It is worth running over the race course beforehand simply for these reasons. In addition, the reconnoitre will enable you to:

- Make sure that you get the best racing line. Ian Holmes will usually run over race routes four or five times to work out the best line up and down (avoiding bog, bracken, rocks and so on), and will do so even for races he has done (and often won) numerous times before.
- Know where on the route there are stiles or narrow, single-track paths that could cause delays.
- Work out which is the best way for you to go, which may not be the same as the person directly in front of you; for example, you may prefer to take a slightly longer route on a descent to miss out a rocky drop, while others will go for the drop.

A 90min Mountain Race

A mountain race probably has the least importance in terms of reconnoitring as the route will be marked and normally there are only a few narrow parts. However, this does not detract from the advantages of knowing the surface underfoot, what the terrain is like, where the steepest bits or flattest bits are (so you can plan your race tactics) and, of course, the race finish.

A 3hr Trail Race

While there is no route choice, if the route is only partially or not marked, a pre-race

A pre-race recce with canine companion. IAN CHARTERS

reconnoitre over at least bits where you know the route to be complicated (for example, if going through villages), or where the path is not well defined, is well worth doing. Unless a GPS is allowed, the alternative is having to focus much more on your map and maybe compass, as you race to stay on route, and doing so will slow even the best navigators down. More likely in the heat of competition, you will just put your head down and run, trying to remember twists and turns on the course. Sometimes this comes off; sometimes not, as happened to a clubmate of SR's who, when in 3rd place overall and closing in on 2nd in the famous Three Peaks Race in Yorkshire, took one slightly wrong turn and went from 3rd to 23rd.

A 10hr-Plus Ultra Race

All that applies to a 3hr trail race applies equally to a longer ultra race, in addition to which, if you are running a route for the first time, you have longer to keep focused on route choice and navigation. Of course, you could just follow everyone else, but how do you know they are going in the right direction? It is not uncommon for a single runner to blindly lead a group of 'followers' off course. Ultra races often mean starting or finishing in the dark and it is well worth going over any sections of the race that you will run in the dark, to gain a degree of familiarity. There is a massive difference between running over a route in daylight and then doing so after dark. Even with a powerful head torch, the obvious trod in the daylight soon becomes indistinct in the dark. Real focus, plus making notes during your daylight 'recce', is worth it.

Doing a recce also gives you the confidence that you are capable of doing the race. Time taken may be considerably slower than you expect for the race, but do not get disheartened by this. It provides useful information to select the best footwear on the day. Familiarization with the terrain and course profile allows you to plan for your strengths and weaknesses, particularly with the climbs, descents and rough/rocky parts of the route. Finally, a recce is useful training.

Food and Drink

Food and drink (other than making sure you have what you need for before and afterwards) are not a consideration when racing for 45min; for the other three races, they have increasing importance the longer the event. Prior to a race, it is therefore important to work out where and what sustenance will be provided. Once you know this, you will be able to determine whether you need to carry additional food/fluid.

A 90min Mountain Race

European mountain races will normally have drinks stations en route, with the bigger races also having dried fruit and similar delicacies on offer. It is unlikely, therefore, that you will need to carry your own; rather, it is a case of making sure you know what and where replenishment is on offer beforehand, should you wish to make use of it (this is covered further in Chapter 8).

A 3hr Trail Race

A 3hr race is likely to have some drink and maybe food stations; however, unlike a road marathon where aid stations are located, say, every 5km, in trail races they tend to be located where access is possible. This can mean either long gaps between aid stations or aid stations that are close together. Depending on where the aid stations are, you may wish either to carry your own fluid/energy gel, or, if it is allowed, arrange for a friend to be at certain points on the course with a drink for you (in most fell and trail races such support is allowed, but there are some events, for example the Lakes 100- and 50-miler, where external support is explicitly banned). Depending on the race location, it may also be possible to pick up fluid en route via streams or external taps (or, in Europe, village drinking fountains). Also common is for runners to hide a stash of food or drink at certain points on the course beforehand and then retrieve them during the event.

A 10hr-Plus Ultra Race

While many runners can get away without eating on a 3hr race, on a 10hr one refuelling is essential. Races will provide aid stations and will normally let competitors know beforehand what foods will be available at which checkpoints. Depending on what is on offer, you may wish to carry additional food that you prefer and know works well for long events. As with longer trail races (see section above), it may be possible to arrange for friends to meet you at certain points on the course (if allowed by the organizers), to stash supplies en route beforehand, or to make sure of natural fluid sources en route.

Two other things to practise nutritionally as part of your pre-race preparations are:

- Your pre-race meal: when and what this is. You may know what you want to eat for an 11am race start, but what about if the start is 5.30pm: do you, for example, still want porridge three hours before?
- What it is that you will eat during the race (we look further at potential choices in Chapter 8).

Pacers and Support Crew

These are really only relevant to ultra races and are not common in the UK; in America, in particular, ultra races allow runners to have pacers (individuals who run alongside them for part of the race). In addition, many events allow runners to have support crew who can provide assistance (food, kit changes and so on) at designated points during the race.

If you are planning to make use of such support, then clarity of requirements are critical to ensure everything runs smoothly and you do not end up, as a result of 'in the heat of the moment' ill-timed comments, losing friends and upsetting those supposedly supporting you. Make sure:

- You and your crew are all clear on what the race rules allow; for example, is support allowed at any time or only in designated feed zones? Getting it inadvertently wrong may well result in a time penalty or disqualification.
- You plan well in advance and give people as much notice as possible regarding the role you are asking them to play.
- Your support crew know clearly what it is you are likely to want, where and when, in terms of food, drink and kit/equipment changes. It is not unknown for runners to hand supporters a long, printed list of requirements and instructions; this may seem a little over the top to some, but better this than angry uncertainty.
- Supporters know if there is a particular way you want things handed to you.
- If they are pacing you, whether you want to talk, them to talk or to run in silence.
- To clarify where they are relative to you: do they run alongside you, in front for you to follow, or behind?
- You say thank you afterwards and if, as is not uncommon, you at some stage lost your temper due to a heady mix of adrenaline and fatigue, apologize and make sure they know you did not mean what you said!

Tapering and Peaking

Tapering is the process by which an athlete reduces their training, particularly the volume, to ensure that they are in the best possible physical shape for competition; it is thus closely and inextricably linked to peaking. Peaking is, however, more than just about being physically in the best possible condition; making sure you are mentally and nutritionally prepared is also critical to ensure optimum performance.

Most runners think of tapering as reducing the amount of training they are doing as they get closer to a competition, and to a point this is true. The best physical taper for you as a runner is an individual thing and something that you should experiment with, finding out, a little bit by trial and error, what works best for you. This is another good reason to keep a training diary, enabling you to compare and contrast the training you did before different races. There are some specifics that we can take from a mixture of scientific research and recorded best practice from other runners, but ultimately there is no one ideal tapering model; it will differ not only for each runner, but also for each race, taking into account the specific personal circumstances at the time.

Before that, here is a quick reminder of why we taper. Training is about putting your body though a heavy training load, giving it time to recover and adapt to the load, and then repeating the cycle over days and weeks. Tapering is about allowing all this hard work to come to fruition, allowing your body to recover fully from the residual training fatigue, but at the same time not losing the fitness benefits it has gained. Many athletes find that, as well as feeling physically stronger, faster and 'zippier' as they taper, they also feel mentally stronger due to less fatigue.

The length of taper For important races, particularly ones lasting over 3hr, a taper of three to four weeks is often used. Positive adaptations can be found from tapers lasting between four and twenty-eight days. Most runners will find a two-week taper works well for races of 2hr plus. For shorter races such as a 45min fell race, easing off over the three to four days beforehand will normally be fine.

Volume versus intensity It is important to maintain training intensity right up to competition, while at the same time reducing training volume significantly (current consensus would suggest by 40–60 per cent in the week before the event, although performance benefits have been seen from both bigger and smaller volume reductions). Training frequency (around 80 per cent) should be maintained. In other words, your taper should involve a reduction in the length of runs, not the number or speed of them, and keep in it some speed or interval work, *not* just fewer slow jogs.

A stepwise, linear reduction or exponential Do you taper your training in a linear manner, reducing the amount equally per week, do you bring it right down in one go or use an exponential model where the reduction in training is small to begin with and then gets greater nearer the competition? What research has been done into this suggests that a gradual linear, or progressive, approach to training reduction is best.

Also, any travelling, especially across time zones, temperature or altitude changes is in itself physically and mentally tiring and should be factored into your taper.

One final point is that while all sports will employ some form of taper, those undertaken by athletes in weight-bearing sports such as running tend to be more severe than those used in sports such as swimming, cycling and rowing. This is for two reasons: first, the latter sports put less of an impact on the body and therefore there is less of a need to recover from impact-generated muscle damage; and, second, those sports involve an 'unnatural' movement, one where taking time to get the right 'feel' is important.

Mental Preparation

All racing requires strong mental preparation if you are to achieve your best possible performance. Mental preparation covers a number of areas, all of which can make a major difference to how your race goes. In the lead-up to a race you need to give time to ensure that you are ready in terms of each of these areas:

- Racing maximally requires a strong ability to suffer, but, depending on the length and nature of the race, this suffering will be different. In a 'short' 45min fell race or slightly longer mountain race you are going to be working hard, at near maximal heart rate, with a feeling of burning and wobbliness in your legs. In other words, it requires an ability to suffer 'short-term hard pain'. In longer races, the suffering is very different. You are not going to be working at anywhere near your maximum heart rate or to the point where lactic acid builds up; indeed, the likelihood is that you will rarely feel 'out of breath'. Rather, the ability to suffer is one of fighting chronic fatigue, sore and stiffening muscles and tiredness, going through bad patches and, with any luck, coming out of them at the other end. There is much truth in the statement that doing well at endurance events is more mental than physical.
- Tactics – what is your race plan? This will be covered further in Chapter 8, but you should, prior to the race, have an idea of what your race tactics are and, just as importantly, how you will potentially react to the tactics of others.
- Optimum performance state. Every athlete has their own optimum performance state: the mental state that they need to be in to perform to their best. This is an area that is very individual. Some

runners (such as SR) become very internally focused, nearly withdrawn, keeping themselves to themselves and not wanting to talk to others. Alternatively, you may become more excited, talking all the time, becoming more gregarious and outgoing (WD is more inclined this way) as you move yourself to your optimal performance state. There is no right or wrong state, only the best one for each person, and it is important that you work out what is best for you and stick with it. Also key is that you recognize that others may not be the same as you. Training partners and colleagues may change significantly before a race; try not to get annoyed or upset with them as that is their way of best preparing for the experience to follow.

Nutrition

What you eat and drink during the final phase before a race should be a mixture of 'nothing new' and maximizing pre-race fuel and fluid stores. For shorter races (under 2hr), this will mean a dietary focus over the last one or two days. For longer races, where making sure that your muscle glycogen stores (carbohydrate) are maximized, focus should be maintained over the last week.

Looking, then, at each of our four races, it is possible here to combine the advice for the fell and mountain races.

A 45min Fell Race and a 90min Mountain Race

Both these events will require near maximal effort and are unlikely to deplete muscle glycogen stores fully, or to (normally) require additional fluid. The key points beforehand are:

- Making sure that as you ease down your training in the two to three days before-

hand, you continue to eat enough carbohydrate to ensure that your muscle glycogen stores are topped up.
- Allowing plenty of time between your last meal and the start of the race, ensuring that much of what you have eaten has been digested. Most runners tend to find that they like to leave longer between eating and racing for shorter races than longer ones, often three to four hours to help avoid stomach problems once you start running hard – any longer than this and you have the potential of starting to feel hungry before you race. Alternatively, some runners prefer to have a larger meal four to five hours beforehand and then something small, such as a banana or energy bar, in the last thirty to forty minutes before they race.
- Making sure that you are well hydrated; it is worth working out how long before a race to stop drinking to ensure that you do not then subsequently need to stop to relieve yourself after the race has started. For races of over 1hr, many runners will then have a final small (250ml) drink in the five to ten minutes before the start.

A 3hr Trail Race

A 3hr trail race is likely to be of similar intensity and effort as a road marathon, relying heavily on muscle glycogen stores to provide fuel. Making sure that these are as full as possible pre-race is therefore important. At one time, the recommended way of doing this was to 'carbohydrate load' by firstly depleting your muscle glycogen stores and then 'overloading' them. As anyone who has tried it will know, this is not a particularly pleasant process, and also one that is fraught with the possibility of going wrong, or leaving you more susceptible to colds and infections.

What we now know is that well-trained

runners can achieve pretty much the same overload effect simply by naturally eating more carbohydrate in the last three to four days while at the same time decreasing the amount of training that they are doing. Here it is worth noting a couple of things. First, when your body stores glycogen it does so with water 'attached'; therefore, if you have loaded correctly, your weight will go up by 1–2kg. Second, eating more carbohydrate does not mean eating more in total, just altering the balance in favour of carbohydrates. Most runners will ease back slightly on their overall food intake as they ease down to match the significant decline in training volume.

In addition, the information contained in the section for fell and mountain races, above, also holds. For longer races, you may find that you can eat your last meal nearer to the start of the race with no ill effects due to the lower intensity of race pace.

A 10hr Ultra Race

All of the above holds true for a 10hr race. Even though the pace of the race means that you will not be putting such an acute call on your muscle glycogen stores (due to using a proportion of fat as a fuel source), making sure your energy supplies are maximal prior to the event is important. Likewise, the lower intensity of race pace means eating nearer the start time is often possible; indeed, it is not uncommon for runners to have a small meal in the last hour before setting off.

Best practice guidelines for pre-race meals, whatever the distance, are to eat no more than normal (especially the night before) – low fat, low fibre/bulk, high carbohydrate, low Glycaemic Index – and plenty of fluid.

For all that is given above, the most important two factors are:

- Finding out what works for you personally

and then sticking to it. If this means having steak, chips and a glass of wine the night before, then fine. (It is quite common for runners to develop slight superstitions about what they want to eat the night before a race, normally based on what they once ate before having a good race. In SR's case, it was always having chicken, until the time when, away from home the night before a race this was not possible; surprisingly, changing what she ate did not have an adverse effect on subsequent race performance!)

- Just as critical is sticking to what you know works for you and not trying out new things. A training partner of SR's, before a major 3hr event decided to eat his main meal at midday the day before, rather than in the evening, theorizing that this would give a longer digestion time. Three-quarters of the way through the race the following day he dropped out, for the first time ever suffering from stomach cramps during a race. This may have been a coincidence, but not worth risking, in our view.

Kit and Equipment

Many trail, mountain and fell races, both in the UK and abroad, have mandatory kit requirements. While these are usually well known in advance, it is in the race organizer's gift to require additional kit to be taken should the weather forecast be bad, or should local services such as Mountain Rescue advise it. For this reason, we would recommend that when going to a race, you always take everything that you might be required to carry – indeed, many runners, including WD, keep a box in the car with a full set of waterproofs, compass, whistle, hat, gloves and bum bag 'just in case'. The alternative is likely to be one of four possibilities:

- You end up having to buy something you already have at least one of at home when you get to the race; this may be just the annoyance and expense of quickly nipping into a retailer selling at the event start, but more likely will cause significant disruption to your pre-race preparation.
- You luckily are able to borrow various items from friends and teammates.
- You miss the race, or try to run without the required kit and get disqualified.
- You 'make do' with another item; for example, as SR once did when finding that a race required full body cover to be carried (these, stupidly, had not been taken to the event as the weather had been very benign when leaving home), carrying a heavy Gore-Tex top and a pair of leggings wrapped around her middle.

The following table gives the likely kit and equipment requirements for each of the four races. As always, these are guidelines only: weather conditions and personal preference will change what is worn and carried. Going to a race is one time when, room permitting, taking more choices and options of kit is better. As well as what must be taken, it is important to find out what must not; race organizers will have differing views as to the use of trekking poles, GPS units, MP3 and similar music players and (although not technically equipment) whether dogs are allowed to accompany runners during the event.

Shoes

Just as, if not more important, than your kit is what you wear on your feet. Here, choice is influenced by:
- *The amount of cushioning you want from the*

Many fell and mountain races require kit to be carried. AUTHORS

Table 13: Kit Requirements for the Different Types of Race

	45min Fell Race	90min Uphill Mountain Race	3hr Trail Race	10hr Ultra Race
Typical Mandatory Kit	Full body wind or waterproof cover Map Whistle Compass		Windproof top Map	Full body cover/ waterproofs Food Drinks bottle Map Hat and gloves Whistle Head torch, if going into the night First-aid kit Survival blanket
Optional Kit	Hat Gloves Long-sleeved top/Leggings	Windproof top Long-sleeved top/Leggings Energy gel Drinks bottle/ Hydration bladder	Additional kit depending on the conditions Compass Drinks bottle Gel or energy bar	GPS, if allowed Additional clothing as required and depending on the conditions Compass Mobile phone if required Poles, if you prefer and they are allowed Small amount of money for emergencies

NB If the 45min fell race is less than 9.6km (6 miles), that is a 'short' race, no kit may be required if weather conditions are good.

shoe – as a rule, the longer the race and the heavier the runner the more cushioning is required.
- *The grip needed* – either for rocky terrain or grass/bog.
- *The tightness of fit* – lots of contouring and uneven ground increase the potential for blisters on the sides of your feet, as does fast descending on good tracks/road for your heels and soles.
- *The size of shoe* – typically, your feet will swell during longer races, so it is normal for those racing ultra events to use a shoe at least one size bigger than normal.
- *The level of stability required* – the lower the profile of the shoe, the less danger there is of going over on your ankle.

In most cases, it is a trade-off between the above factors, depending on personal preference and running style, plus knowing what the race terrain and topography is like. If doing a race for the first time and not knowing the area, if nothing else, it is worth seeking the advice of other runners who have done the particular event before.

Table 14 gives details of the typical surfaces likely to be encountered at each of the races and the likely type of shoe to be worn (see Chapter 5 for more on shoes). It is worth remembering that, ideally, at least some of your training should be carried out on similar surfaces to those on which you plan to race.

Table 14: The Best Shoes for Different Types of Race

Race	Shoe Type	Surface Underfoot
45min Fell Race	Fell shoes	Usually uphill followed by a descent back to the finish Single track or off-path Good tracks, grassy, boggy or rocky, or a mix of all four
90min Mountain Race	Road or trail shoes	Mainly uphill On dirt four-wheel-drive tracks with loose shale surface, forest paths, which are sometimes uneven and broken by tree roots and rocks, plus occasionally grass ski pistes
3hr Trail Race	Low-profile trail shoes or fell shoes	Undulating with more than one climb/descent Surface a mix of roads/trails/paths, which may be grassy, rocky, hard packed
10hr Ultra Race	Trail shoes with good cushioning or low-profile road shoes, up to one size bigger than normal	Undulating with more than one climb/descent Surface a mix of roads/trails/paths, which may be grassy, rocky, hard packed

Warming Up and Other Last-Minute Things

The start of any race, whatever the surface, is a place of weird and wonderful routines as runners prepare themselves for battle. The purpose of 'warming up' prior to competing is to get your body and mind into their optimal performance state for the race to come. While there is some scientific evidence to support the concept of warming up, much of what athletes do is driven by anecdote, superstition and accepted good practice. What is most important is that you believe that your individual warm-up routine will enable you to perform at your best (and a quick glance around at any race will show a whole host of different warm-up routines going on), but there are a few key pointers that every runner should take into account when warming up:

- In rough terms, the longer the race, the shorter the warm-up, so for a 10hr ultra race most runners will use the first few miles of the race as their warm-up, any exercise prior to the gun going off being restricted to specific exercises or stretching. At the other end of the scale, the warm-up prior to a 45min fell race may well be of equivalent length to the race itself, moving through some steady running, specific exercises and faster strides, all of which are designed to ensure that when the race starts you are able to perform strongly from the 'off'.

- Warming up is not a time to focus on stretching or flexibility per se. It is about optimizing subsequent performance, and many runners will have key exercises that they like to do (or believe will help) before they race, either to stretch or loosen certain muscles or other soft tissues. In SR's case, this involves exercises to loosen her back; with WD, the focus is more on her hamstrings and calves. Some runners will include specific drills within this part of the warm-up.

- Warming up for shorter races should finish with a few faster strides, to get your body ready for the faster speed that will be required when the gun/start sets you off.

Table 15: Pre-Race Summary

	45min Fell Race	90min Mountain Race	3hr Trail Race	10hr Ultra Race
Length of Taper	Two to three days to one week	One to two weeks	One to two weeks	Two to three weeks
Recce Focus	Route choice, potential bottlenecks, best racing line	Race finish Terrain and underfoot changes	Where the route is complicated, ill defined	Where the route is complicated, ill defined Route to be tackled after dark
Warm-Up	Good warm-up, stretching, plus fast strides (30–45min in length)	Good warm-up, stretching, plus fast strides (30–45min in length)	Short warm-up, stretching plus a few strides (15–30min in length)	Maybe some specific stretching (up to 10min in length)
Pre-Race Fuelling	Eating up to 3hr before, drinking up to 90min before	Eating up to 2–3hr before, drinking up to 90min before, drink 10min before the start	Eating up to 2–3 hours before, drinking up to 90min before, drink/gel 10min before the start	Eating/drinking up to near race start

Getting mentally ready to race. ANDY HOLDEN

- Of just as much importance as the physical side is the mental side, and using the action of going for a warm-up run, exercises or drills and strides to ensure your mind is in its own personal optimum performance state.

Typically, then, a pre-race warm-up will consist of:

- A period of steady running (10–20min), usually starting slowly and building up in speed – this may be done in race shoes or trainers and is likely to be done in additional kit to that you will race in. The length of this should be reduced in warmer weather and potentially lengthened if colder.
- A series of exercises/drills.
- Four to six faster strides over 100–200m – normally this last phase is carried out

5–10min before the race start, and by now wearing the kit and shoes you plan to race in.

In addition to the above are any last-minute aspects of preparation; this might include putting petroleum jelly or zinc oxide tape on certain body parts to prevent rubbing or blisters, a last-minute drink or word with a coach or loved one.

All runners wanting to race should develop a specific race routine, which they believe works for them, often mixing superstition with best practice; one that covers the length of the warm-up, the order things are done, when race kit is put on and when racing shoes are put on. Having a set pre-race plan will help you switch your mind and body automatically into race mode whatever the race. We would strongly recommend that all runners develop and continue to refine such a routine.

CHAPTER 8

RACING

This chapter follows neatly on from Chapter 7, and in doing so assumes the reader has followed from one to the other, so that issues to do with making sure you have the correct kit, both compulsory and additional for the weather, the best shoes for the terrain, knowing the race details, having recced the course and having warmed up appropriately, are not repeated here.

If you have not been able to recce the course, or it is new to you, then speaking to someone who knows the route, as well as looking at the map of the route, will help you to get a feel for the course, albeit a virtual one. This will be of help in terms of footwear selection, planning your race tactics and knowing (especially for longer races) whether there are any natural water stops en route. Here, the ability to read a map, turning the 2D picture on paper into an imaginary 3D

The start of the Great Trail Race, 2012. DAN VERNON/NOVA INTERNATIONAL

model in your mind, is a skill well worth developing. Doing so well will help you have a true picture of what the terrain ahead is like, a skill that is even more important should you decide to do events such as mountain marathons, which require 'on sight' route choice decisions to be made. This may sound daunting but, like any skill, your ability to do so will improve with practice. You could start off with training/race routes that you are familiar with and learn how to interpret what is on the ground from how it is represented on the map. From there, you can move on to more complicated and less well-known terrain.

What is your Race Plan?

For many runners, their race plan is simple: get from the start, around the course and back to the finish as quickly as possible. Others will, however, have more ambitious aims, from winning or doing well, to doing the same in an age-group category, beating specific other runners, finishing in a certain percentage of the field or maybe beating your own time from previous years.

Race tactics come about from combining your race aim with the type of race you are doing, plus knowing your strengths and weaknesses. For example, in his prime, Ian Holmes was (and still is) one of the best descenders over rocky terrain. At a race such as the Ben Nevis or the Snowdon International Mountain Race he would know that he could give certain athletes a good two minutes' lead at the top and still catch them. Conversely, opponents racing Ian would know that he was better than them downhill, so would make an effort to get away from him on the ascents or, for some, to follow him on the descents, knowing that he normally gets a good line and then try and outsprint him at the end.

Tactics separate the great racers from the great runners; great racers are those who

seem to be able to win races even when they are against 'better' or faster runners by using their expertise and race craft – at times it's a bit like chess while running flat out. This is no different to any other form of running, but with trail, mountain and fell races there are a few more variables to take into account.

What do you need to think about in planning your race?

What is your Goal?

If it involves winning overall, or an age category, do you know who your opponents are and what their strengths and weaknesses are compared with yours? Make sure you keep an eye on them from the start so you know where they are when you start racing.

Best Type of Terrain for you and Where it Occurs

Identifying these factors will help you decide when you might make a break or put an extra effort in, particularly if trying either to catch or get away from a particular opponent. If you are a strong climber, then know where the hills are en route. If you are a fast descender, be sure to know what it is like underfoot so that you can make the most of this. Indeed, your footwear may be selected on the basis of this, at least for a 45min fell race. If you are a newcomer to the hills but are fast on flat, even ground, then make the most of any 'fast' bits en route. In a 45min fell race, the descent is likely to be the deciding part of the race.

For example, in the 2011 Carnethy 5 Hill Race (as shown on BBC2 Scotland), Robbie Simpson was the strongest uphill but he was caught on each descent by Tom Owens. Robbie reached the final summit well before Tom, but it was Tom's phenomenal descending ability that brought him victory.

On different terrain or in a longer race, different tactics may be employed. Although the Yorkshire Three Peaks is a classic long fell race, the change in the running surfaces over the years has now made this more akin to a trail race, with the elite men taking close to or under 3hr. In this race, WD as a youngster, made the most of her descending skills and would aim to pass as many runners as possible on each of the three descents. However, the hardness underfoot is now such that a hammering downhill in the first half of the race will have an adverse effect on her legs later, so she deliberately slows down on the descents and has more left for the final climb and now achieves a better finishing time in this way.

The above is a great illustration of perhaps the most important concept of tactics, yet something that often seems to get forgotten in the adrenaline rush of a race; successful tactics are about doing things in a manner that brings about the fastest overall time or best possible placing, not just the fastest possible for that part of the race. That may mean not going uphill (or in the case above, downhill) as fast as possible; rather, it is about saving something for the following part of the course.

Where are the Narrow Bits or Gates?

If you know a gate is coming up, is it worth the extra effort to get past the group you are running with and therefore not lose time queuing at the gate? Of course, if everyone knows the gate is getting closer this can lead to a sudden surge in pace as everyone fights for the front!

Start Hard?

Going out hard is often needed if the course narrows soon after the start and is more likely in shorter races. For longer races, setting off steadily and coming through the field is often preferable; also, the simple act of running past fellow racers will give you a physical and mental boost when tired.

A 3hr trail race and a 10hr ultra will generally be more evenly paced than short events, but it is still useful to know the course profile. This is particularly valuable if you are having a 'bad patch' (unfortunately, this is something that is quite likely). It will give you an idea of how long you either hang on for or ease off for, until the going gets easier. If the ultra has a lot of hard climbs, then it may help to use an altimeter to tick off the height gain in the same way as mile/km markers may be ticked off in other races. WD found this helpful in the second half of the Ultra-Trail Tour of Mont Blanc during a second night of running. In unfamiliar terrain, but knowing the course profile, it was helpful to notice each 100m height gain and this also acted as a distractor from fatigue.

Walking can be quicker than running when climbing.
DAVE WOODHEAD

Do you Like to Front Run?

Front running means different things to different people; for a small elite few, it is literally that – running at the front of the whole field – but for most it is a relative concept; for example, the front of the women's field, the Vet 40 field and so on. Irrespective of which, the concept is the same and comes down to personal preference and individual strengths and weaknesses. SR much preferred to front run rather than sit with others and then try to outsprint them – playing to her strengths of being able to hold a strong pace as opposed to being able to sprint (not a strength). Others favour the option of running with opponents for at least the first part of the race before pulling away.

Best Route Choice

Is, for example, taking the longer, more runnable route better for you than the shorter, rockier more technical one? Or vice versa – here, having recced or knowing the route means you will have the confidence to take the best line for you, rather than just follow everyone else. For example, in the Langdale Horseshoe Race, after leaving the checkpoint on Crinkle Crags, a common route choice is via the 'bad step', but this can get quite congested if there are some cautious runners just in front of you. There are two alternatives to this route, both at least as quick, but do need to have been recced. We are only talking about seconds, but it might allow you to drop any followers if the mist is down. Taking one of the alternative routes helped WD to her second victory in this race, ten years after her first.

In a fell race, there may be relative choices for some or all of the descent and it is a question of choosing the route that suits you. It is not uncommon in certain events to see the field splitting into two to three separate streams of runners at a certain point as different routes are taken. Long discussions continue about the best descent route from Coniston Old Man in the Coniston Fell Race. An important point is: having decided on your route, stick with it. Hesitation and change of mind wastes valuable seconds and it could be those seconds that separate you from the person you want to beat at the finish line. This is something that may affect not only the specific race outcome, but may also be critical when aiming for points in fell- or trail-running series or championships, where seconds separating the leaders in a race may be the deciding factor in the championship series overall.

Using Drink/Food Stops at Longer Events

Is your plan to grab and go, or to stop and take a short break? There are pros and cons to both. Stopping gives you a short rest and ensures that you eat and drink correctly; keeping moving means less risk of seizing up and you can suddenly gain four minutes on those you were running with, but the down side is that you may not eat/drink as much as if you stopped, potentially risking getting tired later.

Running with People at Longer Events

The reason for doing this may be for company, which many runners find helps them keep their rhythm, or because they are not fully certain of the way. The first year SR did the Fellsman Race, she was navigating by map as she did not know the route. This proved to be no faster than running with a group of other competitors who were moving slightly slower, but who knew the way. After being caught up by the same group for the third time while studying the map, SR decided to cut her losses and stay with them, this making for an easier run mentally as well.

Descending at the Heptonstall Fell Race. DAVE WOODHEAD

The Last Mile

Most of us have probably at some stage watched the finish of a shorter race and wondered why two back markers suddenly broke into a sprint to rival the Olympic 100m final as they made that last mad dash for the line. What is the point of it? Well, maybe their race goal was to beat the person they were sprinting against. Knowing what the last mile or so of your race route is like is important in helping determine your tactics. What is the terrain like? Is it narrow? (The Yorkshire Off-Road Marathon, for example, has a series of kissing gates within the last mile; get to each of these first and you have a ready-made 5m advantage on the person just behind you.) Are there corners? Is it flat, climbing or descending? And when looking at the race route run-in, you need to be thinking, 'How do I make best advantage of this for me, and what are my opponents likely to do?'

Race tactics are a very personal thing, taking into account each runner's physical and mental strengths and preferences. Not only do they develop as you get more experienced, they will also change as your strengths and weaknesses change. When SR first started running on the fells, she was able to run comfortably at sub-6min-mile pace on the flat. With time, age and experience this changed, so that place gains were made over rougher ground, rather than on the flat.

Tactics are definitely something that everyone can get better at planning and implementing. Using a training diary to keep a record of what you do in different races is a great way of being able to reflect and learn – maybe you tried going out hard and it did not work; if so, do you change your tactics next time or change your training to be better able to carry out your plan?

Do you Have a Plan B?

Of course, as with any type of competitive event, while you may have your race tactics, so your competitors will have theirs. Longer events and those requiring navigation also have greater potential for your own race plan to go astray of its own accord. In these cases, do you have a plan B or know how you would react?

Your tactic may have been to start off steadily, but what do you then do when your main competitor shoots off much faster that you? Do you stick to your original plan or speed up and go after them? If the former, you may never catch your opponent; if the latter, you run the risk of blowing up. Here, knowing your body and how fast you can go is helpful, as is being clear about your individual approach to risk.

What do we mean by risk? Going out hard in a race carries a greater risk of blowing up but it also carries greater potential for reward if executed correctly. Running at a more conservative pace carries less risk of blowing up, is more likely to end up with a decent performance, but much less likely to result in a top-class one. An example from SR's road-running days illustrates this well. As a neophyte marathoner, she ran the 1983 New York Marathon and went off fast (especially for her), running with the eventual race winner Grete Waitz for the first 5 miles, after which she had an increasingly slower and painful run to the finish as she faded from 2hr 25min pace to outside 2hr 40min. It was a risk that did not come off. Similar tactics, however, the following year in the London Marathon (going off with the leaders slightly faster than ideal and holding on) brought

The sprint for the finish line, Ilkley Trail Race. DAVE WOODHEAD

greater rewards, with qualification for the Olympic Games later that year.

While it is impossible to list all the possible 'what ifs' and subsequent 'plan B's, most top athletes will spend time before a race thinking through both their ideal race plan as well as the 'what if' scenarios and how they would then respond. When something similar happens they are then not fazed by it, instead taking it in their stride and adapting accordingly.

One of the occupational hazards of races that require navigation, route choice or are poorly or only partially marked, is going wrong or getting lost. When this happens, it is important not to panic and, particularly in longer races, not to lose heart. In shorter races, if you go wrong, the chances are you will lose too much time to be able to remain competitive against your pre-race goals. In longer events, however, this may not be the case, and the ability to refocus on the slightly revised task in hand, put your mistake to the back of your mind and get on with the race, is an important skill to be able to action.

The revised task will of course be slightly circumstance dependent, but will require working out where you are, relocating back to where you should be (or in some cases back to where you were before you went wrong) and then refocusing on the race. Unfortunately, in some cases, the new task is one of just getting back to the race finish in the shortest possible way. Should this ever be the case, please make sure that you always report back to the race organizer. All race organizers have systems in place to account for all those in the race. If you do not formally finish the race nor report back that you are safe, the likelihood is that the organizer will either send out a search party or activate Mountain Rescue to do similar. Either eventuality will waste much of other people's time and effort and is likely to result in the offender

being banned from the race in question in future years.

Eating and Drinking

Chapter 7 looked at food and drink from the perspective of pre-race planning. This section, focusing very much more on what to take, should be read in conjunction with that one.

A 45min Fell Race

Here, eating and drinking is unlikely to be an issue unless it is very hot, when fluid may be helpful. At the 2010 British Fell Running Championships short race, Sedbergh Three Peaks, a 4-mile race with a winning men's time of below 32min, the hot, still air at 3pm on a June day resulted in a large number of competitors experiencing heat stress. None would think to carry water on such a race, but with hindsight it could have been useful, even though this was not evident during the women's race just an hour earlier when it was cooler. As an aside, the corresponding race in 2011, held near Moffat in the Scottish Borders, was quite different when, in near-winter conditions in September, maintaining body temperature was the challenge prior to running, after a 15min walk from registration to the start – a sharp reminder of the range of environmental conditions runners can experience even in the UK.

A 90min Mountain Race

In a mountain race, the organized drink stations will usually suffice but be sure you know what fluids are being provided. If you prefer your own choice of fluid and it is allowed to have it available, that is the safest option. However, if there are a lot of competitors, it can be difficult to find your numbered drink. In extremely hot temperatures, runners who are susceptible to cramp may wish to carry electrolyte tablets to add to water at the aid stations if such drinks are not available.

A 3hr Trail Race

For a 3hr trail race, fluid is important, and in very hot temperatures lack of such may result in failure to finish. The actual type of fluid is personal, with some runners preferring water and others using energy or electrolyte products (especially if susceptible to cramp). Be sure to use one that you know suits you.

A small amount of food is also likely to be beneficial; again, it is important to use something that you have tried and tested, with jelly babies, gels, energy bars or confectionary products being popular in the UK. As well as what to eat, you need to plan when to eat. Most runners will eat (and drink) on the climbs or at the top of hills in a race, while very few will attempt to do so on the descents, for good reason.

A 10hr Ultra Race

Even more so than the trail race, fluid is important and lack of it is likely to mean failure to finish. As before, the fluid used should be based on personal preference, including whether you want to use energy or electrolyte drinks.

For an ultra, the food eaten is even more important. It should be something that will be easily digested and is easy to carry, with chocolate being a favourite of both SR and WD, though this is not practical when hot. Items used for a trail race are equally useful on an ultra, but the best advice here is variety; even chocoholics like both authors have a

Checkpoint and refreshments at the Trollers Trot long-distance trail race. ANDY HOLDEN

strong desire for savoury food during long races. Potential choices include energy bars and gels, dried fruit, nuts, chocolate or jelly-based confectionary, crisps, sandwiches, malt loaf or bananas. Again, all should have been tried out in training, ideally in similar environmental conditions to those you will be racing in. What seemed appealing when hungry on a cold spring day might not be first choice on a humid summer's day with temperatures above 30°C.

In terms of how much to eat, the ideal is little and often. From the first hour until at least the final one to two hours of the race is important (some runners will set their watch to beep every thirty minutes or hour to remind them to eat). It is what is taken in the early stages that is of most importance. If you miss this then it is at your peril! As food and drink will usually be provided on an ultra, check what this is to be and for some this may be enough, but you then lose the flexibility of eating when you want and need to. For this reason, many runners, including the authors, will use a rucksack with side pockets, enabling them to carry food and keep nibbling all the way round, rather than just eating at the food stations.

How Much to Eat and Drink?

We have made mention of the need to drink and to eat little and often, but what does this mean in practice? This next section provides a little more of the science behind what and how much to consume. The limiting factor to getting enough fuel to our working muscles is not how much we eat, but how much can be absorbed (from the gut) and then transported to where it is needed. This holds true for both fluid and fuel: there is a maximum amount that the body can absorb in any given time, although we can manipulate this depending a little on what we eat and drink.

What to Drink

Sports drinks come in various guises depending on the amount of carbohydrate or energy they provide, and there are numerous products on the market designed to be used before, during and after exercise, respectively. All fall into one of three categories:

- *Hypertonic* – they are more concentrated that normal body fluids; while this type of drink provides you with more energy per volume, the higher concentration tends to slow down absorption.
- *Isotonic* – these have the same concentration as body fluids, providing both fuel and fluid at the same time.
- *Hypotonic* – these drinks are less concentrated than body fluids and tend to be better when fluid rather than fuel replacement is a priority.

In most circumstances, an isotonic drink (which contains 4–8 per cent carbohydrate or 4–8g per 100ml) is best when exercising if you want to take in both fluid and fuel, although in the heat you may want a lower concentration to help increase the rate of absorption. If it is fluid replacement that is key, then a hypotonic drink should be used (the added electrolytes and sugar in this mean it is absorbed faster than plain water).

How Much to Drink?

Current scientific consensus is that it is unrealistic in endurance events to expect complete fluid replacement while exercising; rather it is a case of aiming to limit fluid losses to under 1–2 per cent of body mass. We also know from scientific studies that there is a limit as to how much fluid can be absorbed from the gut: around 800–1,200ml per hour in normal conditions. All runners should ideally work out their own individual fluid replacement needs and adjust how much they need to drink during a race accordingly. Here, it is worth highlighting a serious note of caution from the ACSM fluid replacement guidelines (see the final section of Chapter 6):

Care should be taken in determining fluid replacement rates, particularly in prolonged exercise lasting greater than 3hr. The longer the exercise duration the greater the cumulative effects of slight mismatches between fluid needs and replacement, which can cause excessive dehydration or dilutional hyponatraemia.

Make sure you choose the right time to drink. DAN VERNON/NOVA INTERNATIONAL

(Hyponatraemia is an extremely serious condition caused when there is a lower than normal sodium concentration in the blood, and is often caused by drinking too much plain water.)

How Much to Eat?

The current scientific consensus is for 0.5–1.0g/kg body weight/hour, or 30–60g per hour of carbohydrate. Any more than this and the body is unable to absorb it, which may lead to stomach cramps or problems. Ideally, therefore, in ultra races, runners should aim to eat this amount per hour. In shorter races, trying to eat or drink this amount of energy is for most people impractical and unnecessary, given the length of the event and the additional fuel required to complete it successfully over and above existing muscle glycogen stores. Obviously, if you are doing an event requiring consecutive days of four to five hours of effort, then you are, towards the end of the first day, in effect eating for the next day.

What is 50g of Carbohydrate?

100g dried fruit
2 medium bananas
1.5 cans of soft drink
1.5 sports bars
1 slice of fruitcake
700ml isotonic drink
500ml low-fat, flavoured milk
1 round of sandwich – banana, honey or cheese (although cheese may help a savoury craving, it is absorbed slowly so is unlikely to provide useful calories during the event)
80g chocolate/confectionary bar
2 sports gels

Pacing Off-Road

In road running, it is generally relatively easy to maintain your selected pace, and if running with a GPS device, easy also to keep track and make slight adjustments as you go. However, the uneven and undulating nature of the terrain makes this much more unpredictable when running off-road. Predictably, long ascents will be much slower than the corresponding distance on the level, but this is balanced by encouraging speed on the descents (although rocky steep descents, especially in the wet, may be slower that if running on the flat). If you have been over some or all of the route, you will have developed a feel for how fast/slow you are in the particular terrain. If it is your first time in a particular race, then looking at the course record or the times of other competitors may be helpful in predicting your time. Linking this into the course profile may also allow you to 'guesstimate' your time to different points on the route, remembering always of course that different runners do relatively better over different types of terrain.

In practice, getting your pacing right off-road tends to rely much more on your ability to self-pace and use ongoing subjective monitoring as to how hard you are working, how your legs feel and so on, compared with how far you have got to go, to judge pace. What you monitor will also, of course, depend on the length of the race you are doing, with greater focus on overall body fatigue for longer races versus near-maximal cardiovascular effort for short ones. The ability to self-pace is a key determinant for successful race performance. It is something that you will improve with practice and should consciously be tried in training, when aiming to run at a specific race pace.

Other Competitors

The other competitors can be a help and a hindrance! In a 45min fell race, some other competitors will usually be in front of you (otherwise you are unlikely to be reading this!). They may be of help in defining the race route but all are fallible and will have gone wrong at some stage of their career, so you should use them only as a rough check. They may also, of course, take a line where there is route choice that suits their strengths not yours.

In a mountain race, it is sometimes helpful to use the runner in front to 'pull' you up the hill. This involves trying to match their pace and, if feeling comfortable, gradually catch them and latch on to the next runner. If the runner is going too fast for you, be prepared to ease off a little, particularly in the early stages of the race, but in the final mile it is worth hanging on. One tip for doing so is visualizing an imaginary piece of rope attaching you to them, which in effect pulls you up the hill with them.

In a trail or ultra race, you may well know runners of similar ability and it can be helpful to run with someone, so you can help each other through bad patches. WD is far less likely to slow down during a bad patch if there is a buddy at her side. In an ultra, a buddy can again provide support, but the length of the race is such that it is important that a buddy is well matched or you may lose time if you both go through a few bad patches at different times. It is also better to know a buddy because sometimes an unknown self-appointed buddy can chatter away and become an irritation rather than a help. Having a buddy for part of the route helps to share navigation, but always keep an eye on the route as the buddy might become mentally fatigued and lead you off-route.

Buddies can either be friends you have agreed to run with for all or some of the route, or runners whom you end up running alongside due to being of similar pace. Particularly with the latter, while it may be helpful to 'buddy up' for a while, always keep self-monitoring as it is all too easy to end up running too quickly or too slowly for you, as you synchronize your pace with others.

Perhaps the most important message here is that, while runners can use other competitors in a race to their advantage, they should always be capable (unless injured) of coping in the conditions and terrain of the event on their own.

CHAPTER 9

POST-RACE

The race finishes: you slow, stop, walk a bit and get your breath back. What do you do then? Do you make a quick change of clothes and a dash to beat the traffic home, maybe with an added bite to eat and drink on the way? Or do you head straight for the nearest pub for a quick celebratory half or pint? Or change into dry clothes, a recovery drink followed by a 20min warm-down, ice bath and then a balanced protein/carbohydrate meal plus plenty of fluids?

If we are honest, while we may try to aspire to the latter approach, perhaps too often we fall into the former, and occasionally even the middle option! Of course, whichever you do, it does not affect your race performance, that's over with, so why does it matter what you do once you cross the finish line?

Most of us are not 'one-race ponies'; rather, we are habitual runners and, rather like gamblers, once we have got our race fix, we start thinking about and preparing for the

Recovering and refuelling post-race. IAN CHARTERS

next one. What we do, therefore, in the minutes, hours and days after we finish one race does not only help speed up our recovery process (and hence our preparation for the next race), it can also help make the recovery process less painful and more pleasant.

Much of this chapter holds true whatever form of endurance running you are participating in; as ever, though, there are some areas which are more pertinent to trail, mountain and fell running.

Optimizing Immediate Post-Race Recovery

Warm and Dry Kit

If you are anything like SR, then while you feel fine running, as soon as you stop you start to chill, even on mild or warm days, and especially if you are wearing just a vest, which is damp with sweat. If you have had a good race, you probably want to stand around and chat with fellow runners (or even have a little gloat at having beaten them), but on all but hot days you are best advised to change into dry and warm kit before you do so. While this may be subjective, with little researched science to support it, doing so in our experience will reduce the risk of a lowered immune system and hence propensity to pick up a cold or other upper respiratory tract infection (it is a fact that our immune system is lowered in the immediacy of hard exertional efforts, especially longer ones), as well as reducing the amount of soreness and stiffness you suffer in the following twenty-four hours.

The same holds true even if you have had a bad race: get warm and dry kit on straight away, as if you delay doing so, you risk ending up in the medical tent – as was SR's experience after having a poor run, due to being

at altitude for the wrong length of time (see Chapter 12 for more), at the Matterhorn Mountain Race one year. The race finish was cool with a light mist and on finishing and feeling sleepy, SR sat down to recover. Some thirty minutes later, still in her race kit, she was helped to the medical tent and put to bed for a further hour to warm up!

Starting to Refuel and Rehydrate

We know from scientific studies that our bodies are most receptive to starting the internal recovery process (replacing glycogen stores, replacing fluids and electrolytes and repairing muscle damage) in the immediate aftermath of finishing exercise. To make the most of this recovery window, whether after training or racing, you should aim to consume a mix of 50g carbohydrate and 10g protein within 30 minutes of finishing.

While not always the case, most runners will finish a race, if not dehydrated, having a net overall loss of body fluid, which now needs replacing even if you do not feel like doing so. (Involuntary dehydration occurs when athletes do not drink enough after exercise to restore fluid balance.) Because you continue to lose fluid (via sweat and urine) even after we finish racing or exercising, you should aim to drink around 150 per cent – or 1.5 times – what you have lost, over the five to six hours post-exercise. This should not just be water but should contain small amounts of electrolytes (in particular sodium) both to enhance absorption and to replace those lost during exercise.

Many runners use specially formulated recovery drinks for this purpose, finding them easy and convenient to use compared with making up real food, particularly after hard exercise when some struggle to be able to eat. If you know you are likely to suffer from this, it is worth thinking about taking anything that you know you can tolerate eating or drinking straight afterwards to ensure that you can kick-start the recovery process, even if it is little and often to begin with. For SR, after long races water or dilute blackcurrant (which she drinks a lot of normally) are too bland and cause near-nausea; instead, orange juice and lemonade or very dilute bitter shandy seem to do the trick, the near-craving for which can last for several days post-race.

Ideal Post-Race Recovery Foods

250ml milkshake or liquid meal supplement
500ml flavoured low-fat milk
1 round of cheese, meat or chicken sandwiches plus piece of fruit
250g baked beans on 2 slices of toast
Large baked potato and cheese
2 crumpets plus peanut butter
60g cereal plus milk
1–2 sachets recovery drink

Warming Down

Having just run as hard as possible, particularly for longer races, it can be a hard struggle to get back out and run again, although there is good evidence to support doing so, once you have changed into warm/dry kit and have started your refuelling process. Much of the evidence to support warming down is subjective, handed down from coach to athlete. Certainly, this anecdotal evidence, which is supported by the authors' own experiences, is that a period of lower-intensity exercise helps your body (and sometimes your mind) to return gradually to its resting state rather than come to an abrupt return. In doing so, it allows heart rate and breathing rate to return to their resting level in a gradual way and is frequently credited with helping reduce subsequent muscle soreness and stiffness. Where races have resulted in higher levels of circulating blood and muscle lactate, continuing to jog will help promote the lactate's

transport to the liver – this is most likely to be the case after shorter, more intense races or where there has been a prolonged sprint to the finish.

For most runners, a 10–20min jog will suffice; a longer jog may start to be detrimental in continuing to cause muscle damage and delay glycogen resynthesis (or you could do a short bike ride). Obviously, if you have just completed a 10hr ultra, such a pace might be faster than you were racing at, so here a 5–10min walk will help.

Continuing to Refuel and Rehydrate

Especially after longer races, but important after short ones as well, you should continue to drink regularly until you are once again passing plenty of straw-coloured urine; remember, you are aiming to replace 150 per cent of the fluid you have lost. Likewise, you should continue to eat little and often until you are ready and able to eat a main meal. In some cases, especially after long races, this may take some time, during which snacks and liquid fuel/food should be consumed.

Celebrating and Alcohol

How better to celebrate your great race result or new personal best than with a celebratory pint? There is one chain of thought that low-alcohol drinks (under 2 per cent) are an effective way of rehydrating, as their use tends to encourage drinking of greater volume. This is not, however, to endorse heading straight for the beer tent on finishing – as a very rough rule of thumb you should make sure you have 500ml–1 litre of fluid plus something to eat (and have ideally been for a pee) before having a beer.

Any significant intake of alcohol without prior rehydration and refuelling will not only impede rehydration but also most likely delay the full restoration of muscle glycogen levels. Without wanting to be killjoys, here it is worth remembering a couple of other ways that alcohol can impede post-race recovery. First, its action as a vasodilator, hence increasing the diameter of blood vessels, is contrary to either the use of cooling or ice for recovery, or the treatment of acute muscle/soft tissue injuries. On top of this, there is some evidence that those who drink soon after finishing are less likely to follow optimal recovery guidelines.

What Causes Pain Post-Race?

Delayed Onset Muscle Soreness (DOMS)

As outlined in Chapter 2, DOMS occurs after unaccustomed exercise or when undertaking more than the muscles are used to or have trained for. It tends to be most noticeable forty-eight hours after running and is very closely associated with eccentric muscle actions (that is, lengthened during contraction, rather than the usual shortening in concentric muscle contraction), reflecting some mild, relatively benign, muscle damage (remember the hooks or cross bridges in muscles mentioned earlier).

The most common site of pain for runners is the quadriceps muscle on the front of the thighs, particularly after hard downhill running. As most of us can always run downhill harder and faster in a race than in training, even those who train on hilly routes often suffer from DOMS post-race where there is a long, sustained runnable descent such as the

Downhill running often leads to DOMS.
AUTHORS

Snowdon or Skiddaw events. Some runners find that taking an anti-inflammatory tablet is effective in countering the pain, but this is not supported scientifically and, as the condition is not harmful, there is no absolute need to take medication for it. Just be prepared for it. WD remembers an international orienteer, who, despite running fast and hard on many occasions had not experienced this until supporting a friend on a Bob Graham round (involving 72 miles and climbing and descending forty-two Lake District peaks). So unexpected was the DOMS that they thought that they had done some serious damage or had undergone serious injury.

DOMS normally peaks twenty-four to forty-eight hours after the race or event that causes it, and it is not uncommon for runners to find that their quads will involuntarily buckle while standing and that even walking is painful. In severe cases, the pain can last up to seven days, during which time running is not advised, both to help healing and to ensure that trying to run with an unnatural gait does not lead to subsequent injury.

Things that may help alleviate and reduce the pain are stretching the appropriate muscles (those that you have previously been aware of showing soreness forty-eight hours after finishing) or going for an easy run soon after, soaking in a warm bath or swimming. There is also some evidence that ice baths may help reduce post-event muscle soreness.

Sore Chest/Breathing

This is really only experienced after short intense bouts of exercise, especially unaccustomed ones. As a runner, you are left feeling a little tender on maximum inhalation and often with a slight taste of blood in the back of your throat. If you suffer at all from this, it is most likely to be after short, hard, intense races, or occasionally hard (and often unaccustomed) training, such as interval sessions.

The most likely cause is acute and local inflammation of the membranous (soft tissues) in your lung. When we breath normally, as the air goes in through our noses it is warmed and moistened; when we are breathing more heavily and gulping in air via our mouths, this is not the case and the cold dry air dries out the mucosa in the lungs, leading to short-term inflammation and pain (frequently described as 'sharp' or 'burning'), often accompanied by increased coughing and a feeling of wheeziness. Some runners may also experience the taste of blood at the back of their throat, in addition to the inflammation, which is a result of minute amounts of blood being forced through the very thin membranous lung tissues. Similar symptoms often occur in cross-country skiers and other athletes competing at high intensity in the intense cold.

While the above symptoms are common and nothing to be worried about in the context of hard anaerobic exercise, if they persist or occur outside this, then you might want to have a quick check with your GP.

Stiff and Tender Legs

If a sore chest is a consequence of short sharp races, then stiff and tender legs are the frequent repercussion from longer ones, particularly those on harder surfaces. They are the result of a mixture of numerous microtears in the muscle fibres (a minor version of DOMS) plus serious local muscle and other soft-tissue fatigue. While well-cushioned shoes and building up your mileage in training will help, the sheer length of time spent running – during ultra races in particular – will frequently lead to a reduction in muscle and soft-tissue elasticity and hence running economy and movement effectiveness (see Chapter 2): the prolonged time spent repeatedly stretching and shortening soft-tissue structures to bring about movement takes its toll. (A good analogy here is a spring that, if repeatedly compressed, will, after a while, start to lose its 'springiness' as its shock-absorbing ability becomes reduced with tiredness and overuse.) This in turn will lead to stiff and tender muscles, tendons and joints post-race – in particular, the ankle joint and Achilles tendon. There is also some evidence that after long races (for example, our 3 or 10hr races), delayed neural fatigue occurs, which continues to have an adverse effect on our ability to recruit tired muscle fibres, making even walking feel and look like an unnatural effort.

The Lactic Acid Myth

It is not uncommon to hear runners stating they are going for a jog 'to remove the lactic acid from their legs' or that they are stiff and sore due to the lactic acid build-up during a race. Considering the section above, lactic acid gets a bad rap; sore and stiff legs are much more likely to be a result of local muscle fibre damage and fatigue.

From Chapter 2, we know that as you run harder, the level of circulating lactic acid rises (because it is being generated at a faster rate than can be shuttled away and reconverted) until accumulation of metabolic by-products interferes with muscle contraction; at this point, the resultant burning sensation in the muscles convinces most of us to ease up. Once we stop exercising, however, within around forty-five minutes both blood and muscle lactate levels will be back to normal with no adverse effects – a process for which there is some evidence that low-intensity exercise (i.e. a warm-down jog) will enhance.

Minor Scrapes, Blisters and Bruises

Open cuts or abrasions should be cleaned properly with antiseptic. The nature of the events described in this book means that your skin will be exposed to dirt, which harbours a variety of unpleasant germs, including those from animal droppings, which could cause superficial infection or worse, so it pays to be sensible and clean any open wounds thoroughly.

Often after a race, a mix of exertion, tiredness, bravado and adrenaline means some runners cannot be bothered, which is in truth neither clever nor brave. Any delay in cleaning, especially deep, exposed cuts is more likely to result in potential infections becoming deep-seated. Indeed, WD recently saw a well-known fell runner who had a nasty-looking cut close to his eye. Sustained on a four-hour run on the hills in unpleasant conditions, he refused to have it cleaned, insisting it could wait until he got home. In this case, he was lucky, but others are not so and the alternative can be serious: a member of WD's running club ended up in hospital with cellulitis (infection of the soft tissues) after falling during a fell race and not having the wound cleaned thoroughly.

Blisters, cuts and bruises should be managed as described in Chapter 4. If these are small and in a non-critical area, they could wait until arriving home; otherwise, try to deal with them before leaving the race.

Post-Race Recovery Time

How soon after a race should you be back running and training? How long does a race take to recover from, mentally and physically? There is an oft-quoted rule of thumb that says you should allow one recovery day per mile raced, yet we all know runners who seem to race week in week out and often more than once a week. Quite often, top runners (see, for example, Jonathan Wyatt's and WD's respective training in Chapter 2) will use minor races as part of their training, not fully easing down physically beforehand but still racing hard on the day. Indeed, it is de rigueur for those wanting to do well in, say, a 3hr race to do shorter races as part of their overall training programme to improve speed and race sharpness.

There are occasions where runners can produce two extreme performances close together, which seem to go against all we know. On 26/27 August 2011, Lizzy Hawker ran and won the 170km Ultra Trail du Mont Blanc, taking just over twenty-five hours, finishing in the top twenty overall and winning by over three hours. What an achievement that was and one you would think would take some time to recover from. Yet, just twenty-eight days later she set a world 24-hour record, covering just over 247km in the time – perhaps a great example that, whatever science, theory or tradition tells us, and contrary to what we suggest below, the human body can always surprise and produce some unthinkable achievements. What is also true is that the body can only do this for so long or so many times before full rest and recovery is needed.

Time taken for recovery – both physical and mental – is generally proportional to the length of the event, though the amount of ascent and descent, plus the nature of the surface, will also play a role. Let's look at each of our four races in turn.

A 45min Fell Race Unless there is a very steep descent, it will take most well-trained runners only twenty-four hours to recover from a 45min fell race. Some runners will do a race on Saturday, to be followed by another the next day. Even those who decide not to race the following day should be able (assuming a Saturday race) to do a reasonably long, steady run the next day and be back doing hard training within a couple of days.

A 90min Mountain Race This has the advantage of being mainly uphill and, as a consequence, causes limited muscle damage

compared with a race involving ascending and descending. Assuming a reasonable degree of fitness and following correct recovery procedures straight after the race, you should be back into a normal training rhythm after two to three days. This assumes that the race in question is not a peak or final race of the season, after which a more structured and prolonged period of recovery should be built into the training programme.

A 3hr Trail Race The physiological requirements of this event are similar to those of marathons, so the recovery time will be the same, particularly if the course is one of fast, sustained running on hard tracks and surfaces. If the race has been done as a major one, with all-out effort, then two weeks of easy/steady running will be needed as a minimum.

A 10hr Ultra Race It will take anything from a couple of weeks to a month or more before full recovery has occurred and a 24hr event may take several months, particularly if you are not accustomed to such an event.

For the latter two longer events, post-race it is wise to take several days of total rest or do an alternative activity such as swimming, cycling or walking, but without much effort. Subsequently, activity should be guided by how the body is feeling (listen to your body). Start off with short easy runs and gradually increase the time until you return to normal training. If you are still not feeling good, drop back and do other activities (see Chapter 10).

Top marathon runners will often take a full month off running after major events, enabling full physical and mental recovery and giving the body complete downtime before slowly building back into full training. This is a concept that has much to recommend it. We cannot emphasize enough the importance of post-event recovery and recommend for longer events that you err on the side of caution. The alternative worst-case scenario is a slippery slope leading to overtraining, chronic tiredness or under-recovery.

One further word of warning is to watch out for the post-race-euphoria training boost. Occurring after you have had a really good long run, after a short (four- to seven-day) recovery period you feel great and jump straight back into full training. This, in turn, goes really well for two to three weeks, after which suddenly running becomes much more of an effort, runs take longer to recover from and you lose the zip in your legs – all leading to having to back right off in training to recover properly. This was a familiar feeling for SR, and one that took a couple of occurrences to understand and take into account with subsequent training.

Some Thoughts on Post-Race Recovery

Is That It?

It is not uncommon for runners or athletes in any sport who achieve their ultimate goal – be it winning an Olympic medal, a world or national title, or having achieved something they have worked towards for months or years – to be left with a massive feeling of anti-climax rather than euphoria, with a feeling of: Is that it? This might at first glance seem surprising, but dig a little deeper and it is less so. That goal will fully or partly have dominated your life for quite some time; it has been the focus of your training and a point of uncertainty in your mind: 'Can I do it?' All of a sudden, that focus, that goal, is gone, achieved; the world has not stopped and life continues around you, but for you there is a sense of loss, a feeling of: 'So what?' and 'What now?' All this is often compounded by the fact you are also physically and mentally tired from achieving your goal.

There is not much you can do to prevent such a feeling; it is a case of knowing it is likely to happen and warning close friends and family! With time, as you become less tired

and your new goal or challenge is formulated, you will soon be back, raring to go.

Race Reflections

One of the best ways of getting better is to reflect on what you have just done. Post-race (perhaps not straight away but within one or two days), take the time to reflect on your race, and your training for it. What worked? Where did it go right? And where did you make any mistakes? What could you have done better? Look at your training diary critically in relation to this. If you had a good run, then it is likely that your training, tapering and nutrition were appropriate. If you did better than expected, look very carefully at your pre-race preparation and plan to repeat it. If performing below par, look and see if the training was enough or too much, if the tapering was too short/too long and if your food intake was appropriate for the event. Sometimes things just don't go to plan, however careful you have been, but it is sensible to look in case there is something that can be adjusted to make a difference.

Some people find that it helps to write down their reflections as well as their training facts, drawing out the key learning points, both positive and for improvement. SR does this, particularly with regard to navigation points; in effect, creating a checklist of things to read before future events, to remind her of critical things to remember.

Don't Forget your Brain

Carrying out a period of focused training, sticking to a training schedule when tired and to the exclusion of all else, forcing yourself out of the door not just for an easy run but to run hard or do efforts, making sacrifices to family and social life, is mentally as well as physically hard. Many runners will know the feeling, which slowly creeps up in the days when hard sessions are planned, one of both fear and anticipation of what lies ahead.

For SR as for many runners, the period of recovery after a major race is just as much a mental one as a physical one; there is no need to worry about times, about efforts or how long or how far you run, or whether that extra glass of wine or piece of chocolate should be consumed. For her, this does not mean not running, but rather not training; that is, still running but with minimal structure or pressure to do certain sessions.

Building in such mental breaks, at least at the end of every season or after major races, helps invigorate and refresh you as a runner, preventing what should be fun starting to become an unwanted chore. Most will find that after two to three weeks of doing what you want, the idea of having a goal, a training structure and doing hard sessions once again becomes attractive and not a begrudging sacrifice.

Recovery versus Loss of Fitness

It is important to allow the body to recover, particularly if you have a series of events (such as club or national championship events, which consist of a series of races spread over some time). The challenge is to get the balance between training and recovery correct. Thus, the day after a race, don't feel compelled to run, even if you feel fully recovered. Training done on that day is unlikely to impact on future performance and doing something different allows some mental recovery. After a trail race or an ultra, it is wise to have several days of no running: a week or more without will not lose fitness (the effect of the race itself will have been to bank those miles as a training experience). WD regularly has a week of no running after a long race (over 3hrs) but will swim or walk during this time. The difficulty comes when there are lots of long races on consecutive

weekends and it may be that no running training is undertaken in between. Indeed, during heavy racing periods WD may swim more kilometres than she runs between races.

Speeding Up the Recovery Process

Ice Baths As most of us have read, Paula Radcliffe, among others, uses ice baths after races, and seeing runners standing up to mid-thigh-deep in streams and rivers post-race is not an uncommon sight. While there is plenty of anecdotal evidence to support ice baths, there is a limited scientific research base to support them. The theory behind ice baths is based on two interrelated aspects. First, that hard exercise pretty much always results in a degree of microtrauma (small tears in muscle fibres) in the exercised muscles, if not more major ones. Second, the raised body temperature post-exercise means an increased metabolic rate plus increased blood flow. Use of an ice bath is thought to counter this by constricting blood vessels and slowing down the overall metabolic rate, not only reducing post-exercise soreness but also speeding up recovery times – in a similar way to using ice on acute soft-tissue injuries. Current consensus is that ice baths are best used to optimize recovery, for example when you have two races close together. They should not be used when a training adaptation is being sought, as by slowing down the metabolic rate they are thought to also dampen the training effect. Irrespective of the science, many athletes swear by them and, certainly, standing on a hot day in a cool stream does wonders for restoring bruised and battered feet and ankles.

Self-Massage Well-targeted self-massage may be helpful in reducing muscle soreness/stiffness and speeding up recovery, particularly in those muscle groups that you know get sore after racing. WD gets tight calves and

Self-massage: calf. RALPH HENDERSON

Self-massage: tibialis anterior. RALPH HENDERSON

Self-massage: hamstrings. RALPH HENDERSON

141

finds that self-massage reduces soreness. It is important to massage towards the heart; this is further helped by elevating the limb in question, the theory here being that you are encouraging drainage away from the fatigued muscles. Thus, for the calves, this is most easily done lying on your back with a leg in the air at right angles to the body (if you can reach – WD does have flexible hips!). Starting at the ankle, with both hands, gently compress the calf tissues as you slide your hands down towards the knee (if this is painful, stop). Spend a few minutes on each side. This can be done similarly for the other muscle groups in the legs (quadriceps, hamstrings or the tibialis anterior muscle at the front of the shin).

Hot Baths In practice, these are the opposite of ice baths and some would advise against them due to the dilatory effect of the hot water on sore or damaged soft tissues. But they do have the effect of relaxing the muscles, and WD is one who finds them very helpful for minimizing or eradicating DOMS after long races. Caution needs be taken if you do have a soft-tissue injury because the resultant increase in blood flow to the damaged area as a result of the warmth may restart bleeding or increase swelling, as well as potentially delay overall healing.

Anti-Inflammatory Tablets The use of anti-inflammatories after and during events is controversial. Undoubtedly, if there are no contra-indications, taken after a race there will be less soreness and there is unlikely to be any harmful effect (SR will frequently take 200mg of ibuprofen after a long run and having eaten, in order to reduce below-knee, lower-limb stiffness). However, there can be long-term side effects, particularly on the stomach, so it is important to not use them too regularly or on an empty stomach. Indeed, track athletes and those in other sports often use them before competition, particularly if there are several rounds, to enable performance without any distractions from sore muscles and to reduce pain. This latter approach is not to be recommended, something perhaps best illustrated by a cautionary tale. While struggling with sciatic problems down her left hamstring, SR took anti-inflammatories to reduce what she knew was neural pain while running. The wider consequence of this was, of course, the dulling of all her pain receptors, not just those linked to the neural problems, and it unfortunately enabled her to complete a 3hr run with what started as a minor acute ligament problem in her foot, but finished as a major chronic one, resulting in an injury that took over six weeks to heal.

PART III

OPTIMIZING PERFORMANCE

This final section on Optimizing Performance provides more advanced information on training and racing as well as supplementary areas such as altitude training, which can help improve performance.

2012 World Mountain Running Championships. TRISS KENNY

CHAPTER 10

CROSS-TRAINING

As a runner, the majority of your training ideally will be running based, supplemented by some strength and prophylactic training. While there are some runners who do nothing but run, in our view everyone can benefit from appropriate use of cross-training:

- As a way of maintaining fitness during injury: for example, running in water, cycling, swimming, or other forms of aerobic exercise in the gym.
- To supplement running training: for example, cycling or doing stair efforts to improve hill-climbing ability or simply to add an additional, but different, physiological loading.
- As a form of recovery: similar to above, using cross-training on your easy or rest training days if only to give you your daily training fix!
- When you want a break from running: for example, in your annual rest period, keep ticking over physically by cycling, swimming, canoeing or walking but not running.
- As a different training stimulus: giving yourself a mental break from running every day or, in the case of elite athletes, running twice every day.

In this chapter, we look in more detail at the most common forms of cross-training used by runners, but there are others, in particular cross-country skiing, canoeing and climbing, the latter two being skills that you will need to master if you are planning on doing adventure races.

Cycling

Cycling not only provides excellent cardiovascular training but does so in a manner that is known to also be conducive to developing the muscles (in particular, the quadriceps and gluteal muscles) used when running uphill. For this reason, it is frequently used by top mountain runners as part of their normal training routine, and there are many top British fell runners who also compete very successfully in bike-racing events. Because cycling is non-weight bearing, it is possible to spend longer periods in the saddle (if required) that would be impossible to sustain on foot without a significant risk of tiredness or injury. Indeed, competitive road cyclists (along with cross-country skiers where the action also avoids any jarring) are believed to train harder – or at least longer – than athletes of other disciplines, something that is achievable because the load is less than when weight bearing.

For trail, mountain and fell runners, therefore, cycling can easily form part of a normal training routine, providing both a cardiovascular stimulus as well as muscular stimulation specific for running while climbing. It is therefore a great alternative if injury prevents or limits running.

The annual harriers versus cyclists race, when many runners decide to use their cycling skills. DAVE WOODHEAD

Cycling Tips for Trail and Mountain Runners

- Make sure you have the right bike set-up, particularly in terms of saddle height and arm reach. If the saddle height is too low, there will be additional stress going through your knees. Most bike shops will have mechanics who can help you with your bike set-up.
- Bike riding can be used as a substitute for any form of running training.
- If doing efforts, then a straight time substitution is possible; for example, 10 × 3min hard, 1min recovery. It is, however, often possible to do more efforts per session on a bike due to being non-weight bearing.
- For steady, paced training, common

consensus is that to get the training effect of running 1 mile, you need to cycle 3–4 miles – based on the amount of energy you need to do both.
- As an additional boost, over and above a long run – for example, after completing a 3hr run – get straight on to the bike and ride hard for another 30–60min.
- Can be used as an additional training stimulus/recovery session but without the impact factor of running.
- Can provide specific training sessions designed to enhance uphill running ability: in particular, when climbing on the bike standing up on the pedals and out of the saddle.
- If you are using a heart-rate monitor, it is normal to find that, as a runner, your

heart rate is slightly lower when on a bike; this is due to the smaller overall muscle mass used, combined with it being a less familiar activity.

- Aim for a cadence (the number of times the pedals go round in a minute) of 70–90 or higher (professional cyclists will frequently have a cadence of over 100 revs per minute). Broadly speaking, for a given power output, the higher the cadence, the greater the cardiovascular effort; the lower the cadence, the more force that is being pushed through the knees. A higher cadence is also a better mimic of the running action in terms of leg turnover.
- It is often easier and safer, if doing hard efforts, to do these on a turbo trainer (a device that you fit your bike on to, which enables you to remain upright and stationary while pedalling) or a stationary bike in a gym. When training on a stationary bike or turbo, then a one : one time comparison is realistic, especially if working to the same intensity.
- The potential downside of cycling is the tendency for it to tighten the hamstring muscles and have an adverse effect on running speed, particularly if cycling at low revs per minute. If doing a lot of cycling, make sure you stretch your hamstrings and do regular speed work.
- The type of cycling carried out does not matter: road, cyclo-cross or mountain bike. The latter two require better bike handling skills, which might be a restrictor in the early stages for some, but on the upside will help with your overall balance and co-ordination however you move over rough ground.

Stair Training

Not all trail, mountain and fell runners have access to hills on their doorstep or in winter it may not be practical to train on them. In this case, alternatives have to be used. Stairs are readily available and stair training is particularly appropriate for those with access to multi-storey buildings when running up the stairs during work tasks; or, more particularly, specific training can be done on the stairs during a lunch break or before/after work, using them as 'hill reps'.

As well as adapting the hill sessions provided in Chapter 2, the following are some more suggestions of how to use stairs in your training:

- *Fast feet take one* – using a short set of steps (two to three levels in a building), which takes around 20sec. Run up as fast as possible making sure that you only go up one step at a time, focusing on fast, light and quick foot movements – this is about stimulating your fast-twitch muscle fibres, often forgotten by endurance athletes. Take a slow jog-down recovery and repeat 6–8 times, focusing on minimal, quick, light ground contact.
- *Fast feet take two* – repeat the above but this time coming down the steps as fast as possible, using every step, with fast, light foot falls – this will help develop quick ground reactions, much needed when descending on rocky paths. To up the difficulty, use talcum powder or chalk to put marks on some steps, which you have to land on; again, fast, reactive and light feet are key and remember to use your arms for balance.
- *Quads control* – another descending drill, using 20–30 steps, but upping the difficulty and control required – this time take two to three steps at a time – building your ability to control your body and foot placement on landing, as well as helping to condition your quads (the front thigh muscles) for descents. A word of warning:

you are likely to feel sore in the quads after doing this the first few times, but this will ease as your body adapts to the training effect.

- *Power bounding* – using a set of 20–40 steps (enough to get you out of breath but not to lose form), bound up the steps at least two at a time, thinking of good form, driving with your arms and getting a good leg drive. Take a short recovery and repeat 6–10 times, making sure you maintain good form while getting up as quickly as possible.
- *Kenyan steps* – a variation of the Kenyan hill session, this is a great endurance booster as well as helping build the skills needed to move well over uneven

ground. You do, however, need to be able to descend a set of steps quickly to make it work. Find a set of steps that take you 30–60sec to get up, and run up and down this with no recovery. Start with 10min and build up to 20min; you will find your heart rate stays high the whole time.

- *Ladder session* – using a block of stairs with at least five or six floors, run hard from the bottom to floor six, jog down, run hard to floor five, jog down. Keep going down the ladder and, for a hard session, go back up.

There is a whole branch of the sport dedicated to stair or tower races, where competitors race from the bottom to the top

Recceing the steps that formed part of the 2012 European Mountain Running Championships. AUTHORS

of tall buildings such as Tower 42 in London, some 920 steps from top to bottom. As might be expected, there is a significant crossover between uphill mountain running and stair racing.

Other Alternatives

If a suitable office block with stairs, or domestic stairs are not available, step ups can be considered, but the boredom factor needs to be overcome and it takes a lot of step ups just to achieve 500m of ascent. There is also the potential for quite sore muscles due to the eccentric muscle action. If used, step ups should be done using a step that is no higher than knee height. Many gyms have stair-climbing machines, therefore making the job

simpler and the boredom factor more easily tackled by watching a TV/video or listening to music.

Some runners find that training with small ankle weights on is beneficial for improving leg strength. The downside to this, as well as feeling a bit strange, is that wearing the weights has the potential either to alter the normal running stride or put excessive load on to related soft tissues, leading to an increased risk of injury.

Swimming

Swimming has fewer pure crossover fitness benefits for runners, but when done hard enough it will have a cardiovascular benefit

The start of the Great North Swim, 2012. JOHN ROBERT HOLMES

and it is a great form of recovery training, and one used extensively by WD. If you are a reasonably competent swimmer, you can plan a swim training session in the same way as you would a running one. For example, if you want to work on endurance, a long swim at a constant pace would be done, the distance being selected according to how long you want. If using swimming as recovery exercise after hard racing or training, then something more relaxed is better and may range from 1 to 3km according to ability, at a slower pace.

More often than not, a swimming training session is divided into reps. For example, it might be 4 × 400m or 2 × 400m, 2 × 200m and 4 × 100m or 400m, 2 × 200m, 2 × 100m, 2 × 200m and 400m. As with running, you can work either with a timed recovery between the hard efforts, until you are breathing comfortably or returned to a predetermined heart rate.

If you want to do more speed-focused work, then obviously the reps or efforts will be shorter; for example, 25m/50m sprints using a predetermined heart rate as a guide to recovery, or having a fixed rest period. Variety can be added by doing different strokes, arms only, legs only or using floats to enable focus on technique. The permutations are endless.

As with running, many people find it is easier to train by joining a local swimming club and attending prescribed training sessions, which are set and overseen by a coach (also handy if you want to improve your technique).

For those who are less able at swimming, the principles for improvement are the same as for any sport: divide up the time you have available and set yourself achievable goals that get progressively harder. For example, to complete 800m within one training session may be the initial challenge; once achieved, as

with any training programme, gradually increase the amount that you swim. Breaking a session into repetitions reduces the potential boredom factor and makes it easier to keep track of how many lengths you have swum.

Some may wish to do open-water swims, particularly if planning on taking part in adventure races. In the UK, it is sensible to wear a wetsuit. Swimming any distance is more difficult in open water compared with the pool, as you do not get the even momentary 'rest' at the end of each length of the pool, although the buoyancy of a wetsuit partly compensates for this. Do not swim alone in open water unless you are an experienced swimmer or the water is shallow.

Deep-Water Running

Deep-water running involves running in water, deep enough for your feet not to touch the pool bottom, enabling you to continue exercising using a running-specific action, but in an impact-free environment. Normally this involves wearing a flotation device around your waist to provide some additional buoyancy, although some runners prefer not to use one. The advantages of the latter approach are that you cannot rest and have to work hard all the time just to stay afloat, while the disadvantages are that it is much easier to move away from the normal running action to one that simply keeps your head above water and, if doing efforts, you can really only stop at the end of the pool.

A number of elite runners regularly use pool-running sessions as part of their normal training routine, providing a running-specific session without the impact. From a scientific perspective, the research indicates that deep-water running provides a similar physiological stimulus to land-based running. This is something that is supported by anecdotal evidence from users, including SR, who used deep-water running extensively when suffering from a stress fracture and, within four weeks back running on land, won the Northern Cross-Country Championships.

If using deep-water running, the best thing is just to swap your land-based sessions into the water on a time basis; for example, if you had planned to run for 4 miles, run in the water for 35–40 minutes or however long your run would normally take. In the same way as using a treadmill, water running can become monotonous and many runners find it easier to do efforts or mix hard and easy sessions. Here, again, you are best to do a one : one time swap with what you would do on land. It is, however, possible to do longer pool-based interval sessions as you do not have the impact factor to take into account.

Pool-Running Tips

- If using a heart-rate monitor, your heart rate for any given intensity is likely to be around 10 per cent lower in the water.
- Always check with the pool attendants that they are happy for you to run in the water and which is the best lane or area of the pool for you to use.
- Your upper body tends to work harder when running in the water compared with land.
- The non-impact nature of the exercise means you are likely to feel tired but not as sore or stiff as you would after a land-based running session – so factor this into how you gauge your post-session recovery.

Gym-Based Aerobic Machines

Most trail, mountain and fell runners tend to avoid gyms unless they have to. However, there are times, not only when injured, but also when travelling for work purposes and in new locations, that making use of their facilities can be useful. An aerobically based circuit session, with some weights added in, either self-designed or as a taught class, will give anyone a decent training session.

The range of potential aerobic equipment available in gyms is now extensive, as well as standard treadmills and bikes, other options are:

- Rowing machines.
- Recline cycles.
- Step machines – may or may not have an arm action included.
- Elliptical trainers – provide a fully supported running-based action for the lower body, and may or may not have an associated arm action.
- Cross-trainers – with either a skiing or skating movement, plus arm action.

All of the above can provide valuable aerobic exercise; it is important, however, especially on the rowing machine (where it is easy to turn an action that should stress your legs into one with greater stress on your back and arms), to make sure that you have the correct technique.

Many runners find that even with the in-house music and TV, exercising inside and on one spot is boring. As well as using the programmable options available on most machines, other possibilities for helping keeping focused include:

- Seeing how many calories you can theoretically burn in 10min per machine (if there are four different types of machine available, that gives you 40min of exercise).
- The same but adding two–four core/stomach or upper arm exercises in between each aerobic exercise bout.

- Alternatively, racing yourself on each machine to see how quickly you can 'burn', say, 100 calories on different machines.

If you do decide to try some of the above, we have a couple of words of warning. First, we would not recommend that you pay too much notice to the calorie expenditures given on machines, even if they have asked you to input your weight and other data. The figures are no more than a guide, but can be great fun when used as above. Second, remember that any new or unaccustomed form of exercise is likely to leave you a little sore and stiff for the next couple of days.

Hillwalking

Hillwalking can form an important part of a trail, mountain and fell runner's training programme. Perhaps one of the best-known advocates for this is Angela Mudge. An international cross-country runner, World Mountain Running Champion, British Fell Running Champion as well as winner of numerous trail, mountain and Sky races, Angela regularly includes long walks at a decent pace in the hills and mountains as part of her training, to supplement the short, faster, more intense running she does. As well as helping build off-road-specific endurance,

Hillwalking, showing different techniques. AUTHORS

hillwalking will help you get better at moving over rough terrain, condition your quadriceps for descending, as well as providing a similar climbing stimulus to that when racing (where there is a good chance you will be walking, at least some of the time).

Yoga/Pilates

Yoga and Pilates are both exercise-based regimes designed to strengthen the mind and body. While neither will provide much of a cardiovascular or physiological benefit, many runners find that including one or other of them into their overall training programme helps in terms of balance, posture, flexibility and core control. There is a view that having good core strength and doing general body conditioning may improve running economy.

SkyRaces

SkyRaces are those covered by the International Skyrunning Federation, the international body representing skyrunning. Skyrunning is defined as running in the mountains above 2,000m altitude where the incline exceeds 30 per cent and the climbing difficulty does not exceed II° grade (although these are not strictly adhered to, with both the Snowdon mountain race and Ben Nevis fell race having been included as SkyRaces in recent years). The Federation organizes an annual Skyrunner World Series, with seventeen races in thirteen countries in 2011.

CHAPTER 11

THE FINAL ONE PER CENT

A truly winning performance, where you achieve the goals you have set, is about getting everything right, making sure that all the factors that can impact on performance are covered. This chapter looks in more detail at five areas that can help you, as a trail, mountain and fell runner, find that additional one per cent.

Altitude

Altitude Acclimatization

While not a problem if you race exclusively in the UK, if you decide to race in Europe or further afield then the altitude of the race (the height above sea level) can be a major – negative – factor. As we gain height above sea level, there is both a reduction in the pressure of the oxygen that we breathe and also a reduction in the amount of oxygen available. This means that, although the percentage of oxygen in the air is the same, the reduced oxygen partial pressure makes it harder to get the same amount of oxygen to the working muscles as compared with sea level. This in turn leads to an increased effort for all types of physical exertion, including running. We breathe more rapidly and our heart beats faster, both at rest and for a given workload, compared with at sea level.

Most runners will not feel the effect of being at altitude for heights of up to around 1,000m (although even at this height running may still feel harder and benefit will be gained

from spending time at that altitude). Once over 1,500m, however, the detrimental effects become more profound and can be at least partly offset by a period of time acclimatizing to the altitude (just as you would for heat, for example). This should be for a minimum of two weeks, but ideally for four to six, to enable full acclimatization to occur.

For those who are unable to spend time fully acclimatizing before a race, the next best option is to spend not more than twenty-four hours at altitude before competing. While this short time does not allow for acclimatization to take place, it is also too short for the short-term negative effects of the acclimatization process (dehydration, sleep disturbances, various biochemical changes) to manifest themselves. What, in all circumstances, should be avoided is competing in the three to six day window after arriving at altitude, as this is when your body will be feeling the full effects of the altitude but has yet to start to benefit from the positive physiological changes as it adapts.

Altitude Training

Altitude training, as opposed to altitude acclimatization for a race at altitude, is designed to bring about positive physiological changes. The theory behind altitude training is that the lower level of oxygen saturation stimulates the body's production of red blood cells, hence making it easier to train at altitude. This leads to an increase in maximal oxygen uptake, which in turn increases

Jonathan Wyatt training at altitude, Kizbühel. DROZ PHOTOS/SALOMON

performance for a short period when you return to sea level. There is also some evidence to show improvements in running economy, lactate threshold and fat utilization with altitude training.

While there is still limited scientific research to fully support the altitude concept, the practical evidence in terms of the number of endurance athletes who use it to their benefit is overwhelming. There are various different approaches to altitude, namely:

- *Live high, train high* – as you would if you were living and training at altitude; the downside of this is that, because you are trying to run and work hard in such a refined atmosphere, there is evidence that your ability to do really intense training may suffer.
- *Live high, train low* – either through travelling down to train, or more frequently through the use of an altitude tent to sleep in (here the air pressure is artificially reduced to mimic being at a certain altitude), you get the benefit of stimulating the body's red-blood-cell production, without the negative effects of having to train at altitude. However, to bring about a positive change you need to be spending around ten to twelve hours a day at altitude/in the altitude tent.
- *Live low, train high* – current evidence is that this does not provide a strong or large enough stimulus to bring about a significant change in red-blood-cell development.

At the time of writing, there would appear to be consensus that altitude training is of major benefit to most endurance runners; indeed, UK Athletics have a comprehensive programme making use of all three types.

With the advent of commercial training centres at altitude in Europe, Africa and America, for many performance-focused runners a training trip to altitude is now a viable option. Current best-practice guidelines for those wishing to incorporate such a period of training into their programme are:

- Go for an altitude of 1,800–2,500m – the higher end is better for improving base aerobic fitness, the lower end for also being able to do some higher-intensity training.
- Make sure your iron status is good before you go and you are not overly tired or run down.
- Best performance windows on return to sea level would appear to be after two to three days, followed by a dip, before picking up again after ten days – this, however, is very individual.
- Ideally, you need three to four weeks at altitude to result in a significant change in red-blood-cell count.
- The best results would appear to come from a consistent use of altitude rather than a one-off training trip.
- Altitude responses are very individual, both in terms of any physiological improvements and the timing of optimal performance on your return, so anyone wishing to try altitude training for the first time should ideally do so well before a major event – altitude training can be harsh and not everyone responds well to it.
- For some, the benefits may well come from the 'training camp effect'; in other words, not the altitude per se, but being in a training-focused environment with like-minded companions.

For trail, mountain and fell runners, altitude training has two potential benefits: first, that of improving their ability as endurance runners and, second, helping prepare them for races, which, if not starting, often finish, or go up to, a significant altitude. However, as with nutritional supplements, altitude will not improve your performance beyond what your genetics are capable of, but it may help optimize it.

Performance Mindset

Mental toughness is an often talked about, but in truth is not a well understood concept (despite the best efforts of many scientists and coaches), certainly in terms of how you help runners develop it. What it describes is, however, something experts agree is essential for success and forms a key part of having a performance mindset. Mental toughness and an ability to prepare meticulously are key components of a performance mindset, both of which are essential for successful trail, mountain and fell runners.

We have already noted how great trail, mountain and fell runners such as Ian Holmes spend time recceing routes prior to races even if they know them well, and successful runners are renowned for their meticulous planning, checking and preparing for events – kit, clothes, food, route and so on. This is one area where there is a potential difference between other forms of running and trail, mountain and fell running: especially for longer events, the pre-event planning (see Chapter 7) can truly make the difference between winning and losing.

Your mental approach to the race itself can also make a difference. There is an oft-repeated phrase 'if you do not think you can do something, then you won't do it'; in other words, unless you truly believe that you can achieve something, the chances of it happening are very slim. In most cases, this is not about winning but achieving maximum potential in an event, as there is only one race winner. In a trail-, mountain-, and fell-running race, if you have done the training and preparation, having the belief in yourself that your aim (whatever it is) is achievable is really important if you are ultimately going to achieve it.

Unfortunately, during the build-up to a major event, as you taper your training it is not unusual for the negative parts of your mind to start to get the upper hand, bringing feelings of doubt and uncertainty to the fore and negatively affecting confidence regarding fitness or injury worries. This is not uncommon and probably more of us than care to admit it suffer to some degree from such thoughts. Using positive self-statements, being able to look back at the great training you have done in your training diary, as well as how you did in previous events, can all help overcome this. Some negative thoughts are normal and some nervous energy is a positive thing to help focus you on the forthcoming event.

The other key element of a performance mindset, especially for those racing over longer distances, is the mental strength to carry you through the inevitable bad patches. Indeed, the longer the race, the greater the importance of mental strength compared with physical strength to perform well. If you know you are likely to be in this situation, it is useful to develop t echniques to help get through bad patches. One the authors use successfully is acknowledging and remembering previous 'bad patches' that you have successfully overcome. These can be consciously thought about before the event in preparation (if you have prepared and planned for something to happen, then when it does, it is not as bad), as well as recalled during the event when a bad patch hits.

Even if you have yet to experience a particular problem, prior mental rehearsal of what that might feel like and how you plan to cope

with it will help, as will learning from others. WD remembers a friend who was two-thirds of the way round a 24-hour challenge, semi-conscious and twitching, who, after being fed, watered and encouraged, was able to complete the challenge. Subsequently, she has seen a number who have given up on such challenges when they had the physical strength but not the mental strength to carry on. This memory has subsequently helped her overcome similar if not quite so severe bouts of tiredness.

Another trick is having predetermined things to think about as a distraction for when you get weary. Examples here include repeatedly counting to 100 (a technique Paula Radcliffe uses), having a personal positive mantra ('I am strong' being a very simple one), which you repeat, singing songs to yourself or focusing only as far as the next control or checkpoint. Or, as a friend explained to SR, 'When things got bad I kept telling myself that I did not want to have to go home and tell the kids I had had to give up and that got me through the bad patch.' Also useful, as previously mentioned, can be teaming up with a 'buddy' during the race, if only for a short while. Whatever tactic you use, what is critical is that you remain focused on the task and also alert to the route, as well as feeding and drinking.

Training Diary

For us, putting a training diary in a chapter on the final 1 per cent is a slight anomaly, as it really should be an essential aspect for anyone who wants seriously to become a better runner. Most of us can, in the hours and minutes after a run, remember where we went, how we were feeling, how long we took and what the weather was like; but how many of us remember the same detail a month later, let alone a year later? Even at its most basic, just recording how long and how far you run for each day is a valuable tool in helping you reflect on the training you did leading into a race and from there, planning what to do going forward. Adding a little more detail about how you felt – were you tired? did the run feel easy? – gives that bit more information to help you understand both what worked well and what did not when planning for the next race.

It also enables you to put things in context; for example, you may have just done an interval session with the times being much slower than four weeks before, which, on face value, is potentially not great news if you are trying to get faster. A quick look in your training diary shows that, four weeks ago the weather was very benign, not windy like it was today, and you had had an easy day before, not like this time when you had had to do your run at 5.30am before travelling to work. With these added considerations, it is not surprising that your times were slower, even if your fitness is better.

Alternatively, you may suddenly find that you are struggling to keep up with your colleagues at the running club, something you normally do easily. Our natural tendency is to think we are unfit and need to train harder, whereas a quick look at your training diary may show it is the opposite – you have had a great ten-week training period and got a little carried away and just need to back off and have a period of reduced training for a while.

A training diary is therefore a great reflective tool, which can help us review the things that helped or hindered a good performance. The more detailed it is, the more helpful. However, even a note of training hours/distance per session, with race details, will provide a framework on which to review your performance. Depending on how detailed you want to be, there are various other bits of information that you might want to record (see the box at right). By keeping

details of races, a training diary also allows you to see if you have allowed enough recovery time, something particularly important after longer events. Likewise, if you have a gut problem in a race, then pre-race diet analysis is useful. You may also wish to make a note of footwear or clothing used, as a reference for future years.

For those interested, there are now numerous web-based training diaries, which can also be accessed via phone apps.

Training Diary Information

Training Run
Time and distance of run
Route or where you ran
What type of run it was – hard, steady, easy
How the run felt
What the weather was like – temperature, windy, rain and so on
What the ground underfoot was like
What you ate/drank – especially for longer runs
What shoes you wore
What your heart rate was
Other training – strength, cross-training and so on

You in General
How many hours you slept
Morning heart rate (can be used as a predictor of recovery/overtraining)
Morning body weight
How you felt mentally
What you ate – if doing longer races, knowing what you ate on the days before the race can be useful when reflecting on whether you felt you had eaten enough or too much
For women, when your periods start and stop
Details of other stressors – work, family (if you have had a row with your partner, for example)

Do not, however, think of a training diary just as something to consult when things go wrong. When you have had a good run it is worth looking back at both short- and long-term training to see the factors that have contributed to it. Likewise, many runners find that reading their training diary before a major race helps reinforce their confidence, by seeing all the hard work and training that has been done.

Nutritional Supplements

There is a vast amount of information available declaring the benefits of numerous and varying nutritional supplements, but sadly very little proven research to support them. Often the promoted products are ones where, because they are known to be used by the body to help strengthen the immune system, for example, taking more of them is claimed to be beneficial. In most cases, this is not true in practice, with the body having an optimal level of requirement, and sometimes excessive dosages over and above this level can be dangerous. All pharmaceutical products have to go through rigorous and very expensive testing procedures before they are allowed to be taken by humans, but there is not the same requirement for nutritional supplements.

If a runner eats a well-balanced diet, including all the required nutrients, then there is no theoretical need for supplementation. However, if you have any unusual dietary habits – for example, no dairy products, low iron intake, no fruit or vegetables – then supplements to supply 'missing' vitamins and minerals are appropriate. For women of child-bearing age (10–50), there is the potential risk of iron deficiency because of menstrual loss, particularly if they are poor natural absorbers of iron from food sources, so this is one area that may require attention if there is excessive tiredness or underperformance. Children,

breast-feeding mothers and post-menopausal women have a higher calcium requirement, so if there is a low or no dairy intake, then again there may be a case for supplementation.

Many runners (including SR in the past) hold the view that prevention is better than cure and take an over-the-counter supplement as a precaution. If you take no more than the recommended daily amount and the supplements are from a reputable brand, there is no harm in this, even if potentially there is also no gain! Typical examples of this are:

- A general multi-vitamin/mineral.
- Vitamin C and zinc – at times of added stress or lower immunity.
- Iron – for females and especially if eating low/no red meat and limited non-haem iron sources.
- B vitamin supplement – if eating low/no meat and at times of stress.

With regard to the wider world of supplements, the writing of this book coincided with a comprehensive review of supplements in the *British Journal of Sports Medicine*. From this, the take-home message is that in the vast majority of cases there is little, if any, scientific evidence to support the claims made. There are a few exceptions where there is some evidence of a performance benefit for some runners, creatine and anti-oxidant-containing substances such as red cherry juice being two. We would advise runners wanting to try out such products to seek the advice of a qualified dietician or nutritionist before doing so.

There are also those supplements that many if not all runners are familiar with in the form of energy-replacement drinks, powders, gels and bars. While technically the point above regarding consuming a well-balanced diet applies here also, in practice the convenience of use means that such products taken appropriately before, during and after races and training, frequently form a key part of runners' diets. For any runners liable to anti-doping drug tests, the key point to note here is to use products from a reputable supplier, ideally one that batch-tests their products to ensure against contamination, and always to make sure you check the list of ingredients.

Adjusting your Body Clock

The Last Meal

Most runners will, at some point, have experienced the struggle of trying to eat breakfast at an unusually early time in order to let digestion occur before the start of an early-morning race. Ideally, of course, you will have practised doing so beforehand to make sure that you get the timings right.

In a similar way, if you have a race or event planned where you are going to be starting later in the evening and running into the night, when should you eat and what is the best food for you to eat? For example, your pre-race breakfast may normally be porridge, which works a treat, but does it work as well as the last meal before a 5pm (or later) race start? Here, as ever, it is worth trying in practice before the event itself.

Sleeping Habits

For races requiring either a very early start or, more importantly, a very late start with racing going on into the night, you should consider slowly altering your sleeping habits in the week running into the event, if possible. For example, if you are doing a race which starts at 6pm and then goes through the night (for example, the UTMB), if you do not adjust your body clock by the time you stand on the start line you will have been awake for at least ten hours, with at least a similar length of time on your feet planned. The ideal would be

slowly to push the time you go to bed and the time you get up in the morning later and later during the week leading up to the race, so that by race day you are not waking up until around midday. For many of us this is not practical, in which case spending as much time dozing or having a midday kip on the day of the race is best.

A similar process can also be followed if you are planning to race abroad somewhere involving a four-hour-plus time difference (for smaller time differences, you can normally get away without adapting); using the time before you leave to start adjusting your body clock slowly to the new time zone (just make sure that you adjust it in the right direction!). As well as adjusting your sleep patterns, you should consider adjusting your training ones, so that by race day you are comfortable running at race pace at whatever time the event is due to start. Not only will this help familiarize you to the time of running, but also to the prevailing light conditions, which may be dawn or dusk and may mean using a head torch.

Sleep Deprivation

Even with adapting your sleep patterns, taking part in some ultra events will involve racing during the night and experiencing sleep deprivation. For most runners, this should not be a major issue for races lasting less than twelve hours, especially if you did some night runs as part of your training. However, for longer races, particularly when it involves running into a second sleepless night, fatigue and hallucinations may be a challenge. For the tiredness, a short catnap, even as short as five minutes, can help. It is worth considering in advance where these might be taken, as it is obviously better and safer to take them inside with protection from the elements, be it hot or cold, if there is the opportunity, rather than out in the open beside the trail.

Using head torches for night racing. IAN CHARTERS

Hallucinations, which are usually visual, have to be accepted and 'forewarned is fore-armed'. By being aware that these may occur, it should not cause too much of a shock if they are experienced, although the first time you approach a house/person only to find that it is not in reality there can be a little disconcerting. From experience, hallucinations can take one of two forms: you may see normal features that you would expect to see – people, tents, cars, houses and so on – but sometimes more disconcerting are those that can be described as 'not so normal', including wild animals, cartoon creatures, large insects and so on – although when you realize they are just that, they can feel quite comforting.

CHAPTER 12

RACING WELL ALL SEASON

Much is written about training programmes designed to peak at one or two races in a season, or when you have a comfortable six to twelve week build up to a race, but there is not so much advice available about racing well more frequently. Maybe you want to do well over a club series of races, or a national series such as the Fell Runners Association British Championship, which is often combined with the English Championship to give a potential eight races, spread from around April to September, with races taking between 25min to 4hr-plus. How do you plan for that? How do you fit the right training in while at the same time recovering from the most recent race? And how do you switch from one week doing well in a short, intense race to succeeding in the following week in a long, steady-paced one?

This chapter tells, or rather shows, you both how to do this, as well as how not to. It draws on the experiences of the two authors, and in particular WD's 2011 season, when she not only contested and won her category in the British and English Fell Running Championships, but also did the same in the Run Further Long Distance Trail Championships. In contrast is SR's season from 1995, a year she aimed to do well in both the British and English Fell Running Championships, plus the World Mountain Running Championship – something only partly achieved, most pertinently the key goal was not.

How then do you best go about having a successful, season-long racing campaign?

The First Thing is to Plan

What are your goals for the season? Without knowing and being very clear about this, it is very difficult to maximize your potential. There may be one major goal or several, with or without minor goals. It may be a championship series or a specific race, though in the latter case, if this is an international there may be the 'hurdle' of a selection race so that there is then a second race plan to consider.

The English Fell Running Championships requires runners to count four races from a possible six, to include a short, medium and long race. Depending on personal circumstances, runners may want to focus just on four races. Doing (or planning to do) all six provides a level of insurance against injury/illness or an 'off' day. Similarly, for the British Fell Running Championship, it is three out of four races, with the need to complete short, medium and long races to count the maximum number of points.

The counting races are usually announced in mid-November of the preceding year, so this is when planning should start if you want to do as well as possible. As well as putting the races into the plan, it is also useful to put in dates for a potential reconnoitre of each race. Personal commitments need to be put into the calendar so that everything can be considered well in advance so there are no sudden shocks with clashes of dates. To be racing sharp it is sensible to plan similar races to those in the championships so that you can both try out your race tactics and check on your race fitness (preparation – see below) before the actual championship race. Any secondary/minor goals should also be put into the calendar.

The next consideration, once the planning for timing of races and related requirements has been done, is to plan the preparation.

Preparation

For most runners, the first few months of the year, or new season, will be spent building up mileage, assuming there has been a period of recovery following the last season. During this time, many runners incorporate a few races, shorter local trail or cross-country ones, which also help as speed work. Doing races that have been done previously also enables you to compare your fitness with previous years (taking weather conditions into consideration also).

As the first target race approaches, your training should be adjusted to be more specific, taking into account the length and terrain of the event, following the principles outlined in the earlier chapters of this book. Depending where you live, you may be able to design a route that can follow a similar profile; this sometimes requires a bit of imagination, but can make a significant difference in terms of race preparation.

Race Focus

It is normal when racing to want to do as well as possible, to run as hard as you can, to get the best possible time and the highest position. However, as we shall see later on, if you are trying to run well all season, there may be some races where you are much better off 'doing only as much as you need to'. For example, if you are trying to win your age group in a club race series, plus you have other national races you want to do well in, then the key aim for a local race may be to finish in front of an age-group rival. The focus of your race should therefore be doing enough to achieve your aim and, if possible, not having to run flat out. As such you are focusing on the bigger, season-long aim, rather than doing as well as possible in each race.

Review

Once the season is under way, it is important at regular intervals (and certainly after each target race) to review your plan objectively and honestly and be prepared to revise it if things are not going as expected. If, on review, everything is going well, it can provide confidence and motivation to maintain the planned preparation. If, however, things are not going as you hoped, then it is time to consider making changes. One of the most difficult considerations is working out if a disappointing race is the result of doing too much or too little training. Presuming you are a dedicated runner who has followed a well-thought-out and planned training programme, then the chances are that a poor race is not due to too little training. More likely, it is due to too little recovery, or it being just one of those days when things did not all go right. It is much better therefore to err on the side of caution, as it is easier to pick up from not doing enough than from having done too much and then compounding things by doing even more, especially if you are trying to race well over a long period of time. Of course, an explanation not to be forgotten is that others may have done their planning and preparation even more thoroughly! This is when race times may be a more realistic goal rather than position, though climatic conditions on the day will influence this.

Recover

If you are aiming to race well all season, it is essential that you give your body time to recover after each effort, especially if you are trying to include longer (2hr-plus) races in your schedule. If you have done your background training over the winter, then, contrary to what is frequently claimed, you will not lose all your fitness should you take three or four days off, or even longer, after a race (this is especially true for runners who have a solid few years' training behind them). As can be seen below, WD does very little running in between races, instead walking and swimming. Contrast that to SR's example, where an overly enthusiastic approach to training failed when it really mattered.

Getting it Right

The Plan

For 2011, WD's main focus was the English Fell Running Championships, having entered a new veteran age group, but she also wanted to do well in veteran classes in the British Championships. Secondary goals were the Run Further trail race series, though these events were used primarily to build up mileage. The same approach applied to the Lakeland Classic series (a series of long races in the Lakes), which is a regular secondary goal as were the Three Peaks and Lake District Mountain Trial events. A 'fun' goal was to do the Snowdon, Scafell Pike and Ben Nevis races in the same season (the highest peaks in each country), having never done the first two of these races before. Another fun goal was to do sixty races in the year, those races outside the main goals being

used as training races or fulfilling the secondary goals.

The Preparation

After a total rest for two months from November 2010, WD's base fitness was near an all-time low at the beginning of 2011. This was evidenced in the Kendal Winter League cross-country races, which were used both as speed training and to compare times with previous years. This was supplemented with cross-training of swimming, spinning and weight circuits. Throughout the year, reconnoitres (recces) were done for all the fell-running championship races, this being used as training or, in some cases, were done walking during a recovery phase after a race.

The Season

The planning and preparation worked well, securing the FV55 and FV60 title in the English Fell Running Championships and the FV50 in the British Fell Running Championships. The remainder of the year allowed secondary goals to be achieved, accruing the most female points for the informal three-race series of Snowdon, Ben Nevis and Scafell Pike, completing the Lakeland Classics and Run Further series, securing age-group victories. A twenty-eighth completion of the Three Peaks was achieved. Another secondary goal, to do well at the Lake District Mountain Trial, also came to fruition, securing WD's best position ever, after twenty-six appearances in the race and thirty-three years after doing her first one. Sixty races were completed in the year, well before the deadline, allowing a relaxed SR and WD to complete the A course in the Original Mountain Marathon.

The Reflection

Was this just a 'lucky' year? Perhaps it was a more carefully planned and prepared year than previous ones, but not too dissimilar from

Table 16: WD's Trail-, Mountain- and Fell-Running Season

Month	Week I	Week 2	Week 3	Week 4	Week 5	Training Comment
January	KWL	KWL	KWL	XC race LWDA event		As expected, slow start but surprised with reasonable times by week 4
February		KWL Carnethy5 (trg)	KWL Loughrigg–Silverhowe (trg)	KWL High Cup Nick (trg)	KWL	Race times all acceptable
March		(1°) Long Mynd Valleys (LMV) Eng (M) (recce Nov 2011)	(2°) Run Further (S)	(2°) Run Further (L)		Pleasing time and position at LMV. Slow times at Run Further events, reflecting lack of mileage
April		(2°) Run Further (M)		(2°) Three Peaks		Disappointing Run Further event, suffering in the heat
May		(1°) Mearley Clough (MC) Eng (S) (recce × 2, April, May)		Jura (trg)		Pleasing result at MC and Jura
June	(1°/2°) Duddon Valley (DV) Eng (L) (LC) (recce April)	(2°) Run Further (S)		(1°) Loughrigg–Silverhowe (LS) Eng (M) (recce × 3, April, May, June)		Good result at DV and remarkably so the next day at the Run Further event. Disappointing LS result reflecting either under-recovery from high-mileage racing at start of month or lack of racing edge after 3wk of no racing
July	(1°) Y Aran Br (M)		(F) Snowdon	(1°) Whittle Pike Eng (S) (recce × 2, June, July)		Good results, being 1st in age category at all races
August		(2°) Borrowdale (Bo) (LC)		(1°) Sedburgh Hills (SH) Br/Eng (L)		Good result at Bo but limited by cramp at SH
September	(F) Ben Nevis (Devil's Beef Tub recce)	(1°) Devil's Beef Tub Br (S) (2°) LDMT		(2°) Three Shires (LC)	(F) Scafell Pike	Good results, time and position, in all races
October		(2°) Langdale (LC)		OMM		Moderate and more severe injury in last 2 events, but completed

Key: 1° = primary goal; 2° = secondary goal; Br = British Championship fell race; Eng = English Championship fell race; F = fun goal; KWL = Winter League races; L = long; LC = Lakeland Classic; LDMT = Lake District Mountain Trial; LDWA = Long Distance Walkers Association; M = medium; OMM = Original Mountain Marathon; S = short; trg = training race.

others when similar results have been achieved in the veteran classes of fell-running championships, the Lakeland Classics, Run Further series, Three Peaks and Lake District Mountain Trial. For some, this would be too many races. This is where knowing your body helps. During heavy racing periods, weekly non-racing mileage was low or zero, with swimming being used both for maintaining cardiovascular fitness and as 'recovery' exercise.

Key Lessons

1. Plan your season, races, training and other events/occasions well in advance.
2. Review how things are going on a regular basis.
3. Do not be afraid to change things, especially to err on the side of caution and ease back.
4. Give your body time to recover between hard races.
5. Be clear about what you goal is – this may mean not racing flat out.

Getting it Wrong

The Plan

For the previous two seasons, SR had focused her training on two main races: the Three Peaks (a 24-mile race held in April), an event for which she was the course record holder and the World Mountain Running Championships (the sport's major international event held in September over 8km), where she had finished second in 1992 and still had ambitions of doing better. In 1995, the World Mountain Running Championships was to be held in Edinburgh on a course well suited to SR's strengths, therefore offering her the best possible opportunity to achieve her goal. She also decided, as a secondary but new challenge, to target the British and English Fell Running Championships, something she had not done before.

The Preparation

Unlike WD, SR tended to keep herself at a reasonable level of fitness all year round. The period November 1994 to March 1995 was spent following a fairly classic endurance runner's training programme, similar to those she had followed in previous years: 60–80 miles a week, one long run (2hr-plus) one short speed session, one longer speed endurance session (see Chapter 2 for an example week's training). The latter often took the form of a cross-country or trail/fell race. Things mainly went well during this time, although the training volume often meant racing on heavy- or tired-feeling legs.

The Season

The secondary goals were achieved, with SR winning the British and English Championships. She also won every race she ran during the year, except the one that really mattered: her primary goal of the World Championships. The planning for the training programme was fine in theory (longer runs in the early part of the season, then switching to shorter, faster work, with a focus on hills and biking for leg strength), but its execution did not give enough attention to recovery. Nor were the warning signs picked up in training; for example, SR notes in her training diary the Saturday after winning the World Trial:

> First two efforts felt very easy (a series of 5 × 1 mile); after that, times went down and heart rate stayed down, so not going as well as I should be, hopefully just a tired Saturday session.

After this, of course, Sarah started to feel tired and light-headed, symptoms that she had experienced six years previously when she suffered from a period of under-recovery/overtraining. A focus on rest and

Table 17. SR's Trail-, Mountain-, and Fell-Running Season

Month	Week 1	Week 2	Week 3	Week 4	Week 5	Training Comment
January	80 miles 3 × session 1 × long run	Boulsworth (trg) 71 miles 1 × session 1 long run	83 miles 3 × session 1 × long run	83 miles 3 × session 1 × long run	Stanbury (trg) 1 × session 1 × long run	Good, solid block of training
February	Ogden Moors (trg) 76 miles 1 × session 1 × long run	Rossendale Way Relay (trg) 84 miles 2 × session 1 × long run	80 miles 1 × session	WWW relay race 79 miles 1 × session 1 × long run	82 miles 2 × session 1 × long run	Running well, great training
March	Ovenden (trg) 66 miles 1 × session 1 × long run	69 miles 1 × session (recce Edale)	69 miles 1 × session 1 × long run	(2°) Edale Skyline Br/Eng (L) 72 miles 1 × session		Although 1st, struggled at the end of Edale, feeling light-headed
April	80 miles 2 × session 1 × long run	Broughton Hall (trg) 82 miles 1 × session 1 × long run	76 miles 2 × session 1 × long run	(2°) Kinder Downfall Eng (M) (2°) Struc a Choin Br (L) 72 miles		Easy week, then decent block of training (with hindsight, too decent) Both championship races won but no zip in legs
May	53 miles	101 miles 1 × session 1 × long run (1 × recce Duddon)	70 miles 2 × session	67 miles 1 × session 1 × long run	Dodd Fell (trg) (2°) Duddon Br/Eng (L) 84 miles 1 × long run	Easy at the start of the month, but tired later on
June	Badgerstone relay (trg) 62 miles 1 × session	(2°) Buckden Pike Eng (S) 1 × session 1 × long run	(2°) Moffat Br (M) 1 × session	48 miles 1 long run (recce Wo course)		Focus moved to more speed-based training. Turbo sessions on bike introduced Shorter hill efforts Tired at the end of the month and struggled at Moffat, although still won
July	Beamsley (trg) 81 miles 2 × session 1 × long run	(2°) Kinniside Eng (M) 82 miles 1 × session 1 × long run	76 miles 1 × session 1 × long run	80 miles 2 × long run		Much better race at Kinniside Travel to Canada in the last week
August	In Canada 10km trial race (trg) 65 miles	Canada/home 69 miles 2 × session	(1°) Wo trial 71 miles 1 × session 1 × long run	82 miles 2 × session 1 × long run	77 miles 2 × session (one on turbo) 1 × long run	First two weeks in Canada Great run at the trial but pushed too hard, with hindsight Did too much post the trial, diary notes my heart rate down and feeling tired
September	67 miles 1 × session	(1°) Wo 60 miles	(2°) Dalehead Eng (S) 60 miles	64 miles		Tired and dizzy in the week before the Wo, – even with rest and sleep had my worse ever run at the Wo (12th), washed out physically and mentally A week of recovery running brought me round
October	Ian Hodgson relay 70 miles	85 miles 1 × long run	FRA relay Withins Skyline (trg) 77 miles 1 × session	82 miles 1 × session 1 × long run	KIMM	Running well all month

Key: 1° = primary goal; 2° = secondary goal; Br = British Championship fell race; Eng = English Championship fell race; F = fun goal; FRA = Fell Runners Association; KIMM = Karrimor International Mountain Marathon; L = long; M = medium; S = short; trg = training race; Wo = World Championship Mountain race; session = hard/speed session.

sleep helped, but not enough of either was obtained, and on race day SR recorded her lowest-ever position at a World Mountain Running Championship event. Despite starting as she planned and running comfortably with the leaders, she faded, finishing in twelfth place and the second-fastest English runner (50sec behind the person she had beaten by 50sec only three weeks before), feeling wiped out physically and mentally. A further week of easy running was enough to ensure that SR was able to recover sufficiently for the final Championship race of the season one week later, a short one where she won. The end of the year saw SR running really well in the fell-running relay events, as her fitness was finally allowed to show.

The Reflection

Post-season reflection refers too often to running tired and with heavy legs in SR's training dairy from the time. At the time, SR's physical ability meant that she was able to win all the domestic races without potentially being as fresh as possible and hence just kept going until too late when it really mattered – the World Championships. Objectively, she was not smart, getting caught into a classic training hard/feeling tired/feeling slow and low/need to train harder and not being able to see her way out of it (during the 1995 season SR was self-coached (badly), something she planned to change the following year, knowing that she needed someone to make her ease back). At the same time, she did not take into account the potential negative effect of non-running-based stressors such as a work conference the week before the World Championship, combined with the added pressure of a major home international where she was expected to do well.

Interestingly, SR's reflection of the time is one of: 'not anger because I could not have done any more' – which with hindsight is true,

but she could have done less. There is much truth in the saying 'it is not about training hard but about training smart'.

Key Mistakes

1. Trying to continue to maintain a heavy training programme while racing – this may have worked in previous years, but did not when having a greater number of target races in the season, in particular not reducing her weekly mileage and her long runs post-Duddon (because she enjoyed doing them).
2. Trying to win every race well, not just doing what was needed to win the series (SR went into each of the Championship races wanting to win in the best possible time, not thinking what was the optimal number of races to do given the bigger goal of the World Championship).
3. Not listening to what her body was telling her and keeping pushing hard. The World Championship trial showed that SR was in great shape, as did her training, so it should not have been a time to 'push on' with training, rather time to 'fine-tune and sharpen up'.
4. Not using a coach/objective other as a sounding board.

Summary

Racing well all season is not easy, but with careful planning and preparation it can be done. What the plan looks like will be different for every runner as a result of different goals, different strengths, weaknesses and personal circumstances, but having a plan and regularly reviewing it objectively (and revising if needed) allows for a sensible and potentially successful season – after which, of course, a post-season review will help to ensure that the next year is even better.

INDEX

NOTES

NOTES

RELATED TITLES
FROM CROWOOD

High Performance
Long-Distance Running

David Sunderland

ISBN 978 1 84797 245 3
160pp, 170 illustrations

Improve Your Marathon
and Half-Marathon Running

David Chalfen

ISBN 978 1 84797 390 0
144pp, 100 illustrations

The Marathon and
Half-Marathon

Graeme Hilditch

ISBN 978 1 86126 963 8
176pp, 130 illustrations

Off-Road Running

Sarah Rowell

ISBN 978 1 86126 523 4
144pp, 40 illustrations

In case of difficulty ordering, contact the Sales Office:

The Crowood Press
Ramsbury
Wiltshire
SN8 2HR
UK

Tel: 44 (0) 1672 520320
enquiries@crowood.com
www.crowood.com